Essentials of Business Communication

(INCLUDING SKILL DEVELOPMENT)

As per New Syllabus for Third Semester, B.Com
Bangalore University w.e.f 2005-06

Prof. H. R. APPANNAIAH
Former Dean, Surana P.G.Centre,
Former Director, SRN Adarsha College, Bangalore,
Former Principal, P.A. College, Tiptur,
Founder President,
Federation of Teachers' Council of
Commerce and Management in Karnataka

Dr. P. N. REDDY
Director, K.K.E.C.S. Institute of
Management, Bangalore.
Former Dean & Chairmen,
Department of P.G. Studies in
Commerce and Management,
Bangalore University.

GOPALAKRISHNA
Faculty, M.B.A. Department
Surana P.G. Centre, Kengeri,
Bangalore- 60

Himalaya Publishing House

MUMBAI • NEW DELHI • NAGPUR • BENGALURU • HYDERABAD • CHENNAI • PUNE • LUCKNOW • AHMEDABAD • ERNAKULAM • BHUBANESWAR • INDORE • KOLKATA • GUWAHATI

First Edition : 2006
Second Edition : 2008
Third Edition : 2009
Fourth Edition : 2011
Fifth Edition : 2012

Published by : Mrs. Meena Pandey for **Himalaya Publishing House Pvt. Ltd.,**
"Ramdoot", Dr. Bhalerao Marg, Girgaon, **Mumbai - 400 004.**
Phone: 022-23860170/23863863, Fax: 022-23877178
E-mail: himpub@vsnl.com; Website: www.himpub.com

Branch Offices :

New Delhi : "Pooja Apartments", 4-B, Murari Lal Street, Ansari Road, Darya Ganj, New Delhi - 110 002. Phone: 011-23270392, 23278631; Fax: 011-23256286

Nagpur : Kundanlal Chandak Industrial Estate, Ghat Road, Nagpur - 440 018. Phone: 0712-2738731, 3296733; Telefax: 0712-2721215

Bengaluru : No. 16/1 (Old 12/1), 1st Floor, Next to Hotel Highlands, Madhava Nagar, Race Course Road, Bengaluru - 560 001. Phone: 080-32919385; Telefax: 080-22286611

Hyderabad : No. 3-4-184, Lingampally, Besides Raghavendra Swamy Matham, Kachiguda, Hyderabad - 500 027. Phone: 040-27560041, 27550139; Mobile: 09390905282

Chennai : No. 8/2, Modley 2nd Street, Ground Floor, T. Nagar, Chennai - 600 017. Phone: 044-28144004/28144005; Mobile: 09345345051

Pune : First Floor, "Laksha" Apartment, No. 527, Mehunpura, Shaniwarpeth Near Prabhat Theatre), Pune - 411 030. Phone: 020-24496323/24496333; Mobile: 09370579333

Lucknow : Jai Baba Bhavan, Church Road, Near Manas Complex and Dr. Awasthi Clinic, Aliganj, Lucknow - 226 024 (U.P.). Phone: 0522-2339329, 4068914; Mobile: 09307501550

Ahmedabad : 114, "SHAIL", 1st Floor, Opp. Madhu Sudan House, C.G. Road, Navrang Pura, Ahmedabad - 380 009. Phone: 079-26560126; Mobile: 09377088847

Ernakulam : 39/104 A, Lakshmi Apartment, Karikkamuri Cross Rd., Ernakulam, Cochin - 622011, Kerala. Phone: 0484-2378012, 2378016; Mobile: 09344199799

Bhubaneswar : 5 Station Square, Bhubaneswar - 751 001 (Odisha). Phone: 0674-2532129, Mobile: 09338746007

Indore : Kesardeep Avenue Extension, 73, Narayan Bagh, Flat No. 302, IIIrd Floor, Near Humpty Dumpty School, Indore - 452 007 (M.P.). Mobile: 09301386468

Kolkata : 108/4, Beliaghata Main Road, Near ID Hospital, Opp. SBI Bank, Kolkata - 700 010, Phone: 033-32449649, Mobile: 09910440956

Guwahati : House No. 15, Behind Pragjyotish College, Near Sharma Printing Press, P.O. Bharalumukh, Guwahati - 781009, (Assam). Mobile: 09883055590, 09883055536

DTP by : **Sri Siddhi Softtek**
Bengaluru

Printed at : Roshan Printers, Bengaluru. On behalf of HPH.

PREFACE

Sound Decision-making is the vital function of any management. In decision-making process communication plays a major role. It is a key factor. Communication may be oral or written. It is also expressed in the form of body language. But in a business or any other structured activity, written communication is the only mode adopted for effective communication. In communication process, language is the main vehicle. In business enterprises, time being very precious, effective language has to be used for effective communication. Language should be crisp and catch the minds of readers quickly. Business communication covers the drafting of wide variety of business letters.

In this title, we have dealt with fundamentals of business communication for various situations. The chapter 'Structure of Business Letters' deals with how business letters must be structured. Chapter 'Accounts Correspondence' illustrates various types of letters with respect to the accounts and financial transactions, correspondence with banks, provident fund, insurance companies and other similar institutions. The chapter 'Purchase Correspondence' explains the communication process in connection to call for tenders and quotations, and other similar purchase transactions. The chapter 'Sales Correspondence' deals with drafting of literature for sales, product launch, communication with dealers and agents, and other similar activities.

In this book, meaningful description of drafting each type of letter is given. Specimen letters for each and every type dealt is exhibited for correct understanding of the type to be drafted. The appropriate language to be used is also depicted in specimens. Written in a simple but effective language, this work serves the needs of students and learners who are involved in drafting business letters. We wish that this work serves the needs of students to cover their curriculum.

It is our bounden duty to remember the great soul Sri. D.P. Pandeyji who departed from us for heavenly abode recently. As a publisher, he was a great source of inspiration to bring out our titles under HPH banner. "May his soul rest in peace". We thank Sriyuths, K.N. Pandey, Anuj Pandey, Niraj Pandey and Vijay Pandey for their continuing support in publishing our titles. We also thank HPH staff for their efforts in promoting our book.

Prof. H.R. Appannaiah,
Dr. P.N. Reddy,
D.S. Gopala Krishna.

CONTETS

CHAPTER 1

INTRODUCTION AND IMPORTANCE

- Introduction
- Importance of Business Communication
- Communication in Management
- Communication - Its Scope
- Communication and Decision - making
- Systematic Information - Its Criteria or Principles
- Vertical and Horizontal Types of Communication

INTRODUCTION

Human beings have a special privilege to transmit their thoughts through words, sounds letters, signs, pictures and symbols. Thoughts represent ideas. Sounds produced and symbols used are called language. Both the *sender* and the *receiver* of information are necessary to exchange their thoughts. Thus, the processes of transmission and retransmission of ideas and corresponding responses are called Language. Language is a vehicle of thought among people. Language means use of meaningful words to convey what one feels to another. Thinking and conveying through sounds, alphabets and words mutually is the unique feature of persons in human society called "communication". In the world of animals, human beings top the list entirely due to their gift of nature of interchange of ideas, through their ability and dexterity to use understandable language or communication. It is derived from Latin origin COMMUNIS meaning common.

Colloquially, communication is taken to mean correspondence. Correspondence is the written expression of one's message or feelings concerning matters of personal interest or between individuals, firms or companies on matters of trade and commerce. The purpose of letter writing is to pass on the information to the recipient without personal contact. Written words convey the meaning and feeling of the message. Clarification or emphasis is not possible to be converted as in conversation. Expression in conversation is much signified through gestures and inflection of voice. Absence of physical person in written correspondence is the main demerit seen between correspondence and personal communication. In fact, communication is a big modern term used to denote all wings and facets of contact, oral or written. But still the significance attached to the correspondence denoting written communication has not declined or vanished. "Letters were handwritten, often in a beautiful copper plate script and in content they were urbane, felicitous and one must admit, often verbose, (James Stephenson). Constant increase in the size of correspondence, invention of office machines like typewriter, stencil copier stenographic machines, duplicating, imprinting, processing, computing accounting and tabulating machines along with punched card machines, electronic computers, dictating machines, mailing machines, addressing, adding, listing, book–keeping , letter opening, folding, franking, time recording and cheque–writing machines and so on and so forth have contributed much to the case of correspondence and communication. Quickening tempo of business, in a way, has taken away the chief need of letter–writing. Time honoured commercial letters were full of repeated phrases and expressions coined in course of mercantile dealings. Because of ill–usage, they became meaningless. Use of such expressions are now deemed clumsy and senseless. Liberal and indiscriminate use of such expressions came to support the rejection of "commercialise of Jargon". Time factor is prominent in modern business. Prolonged passage conveys no meaningful message. More than the regal and flowery words and styles, precise information in the shortest possible time should be conveyed to the recipients of letters.

IMPORTANCE OF BUSINESS COMMUNICATION

Communication is elementary in a civilised society. Unlike royal couriers, agents and servants who used to carry the message engraved on leaves or metal sheet, modern network of communication media is astonishing and superb. Increase in the volume and extent of business is a major reason for fast development in the field of communication. Clear and accurate communication is always fruitful to merchants, producers, advocates, bankers and others. Every letter has a purpose behind it. Receiver of letter reacts soon when there is a clear presentation of ideas in it. Carefully chosen words will always be appreciated. Simple and appropriate words used in communication will fetch the writer, the expected fruit. Proper arrangement of words, clarity in thought, frank and factual information will pave the way for clear–writing. Failure or success in business may be often due to carelessness of effective communication with the outside world. Indecency may ruin the business itself. Carrying out the business transactions, settlement of dealings and provision of dependable documents for subsequent reference etc. will be the outcome of communication channel to be determined. Competitive market expects a clear–cut communication. A badly worded letter will baffle the business. Unduly long letter will not attract the attention of potential customers. Effective correspondence will add to the beauty of business entity. A timely response with a sense of perfection may bring in large sales in the organisation concerned. A letter with a good beginning will certainly press the reader to fully go through the correspondence. Clear business, prompt settlement of customer's account and earning as well as retaining a band of loyal customers may be entirely due to a series a well worded letters. Success of every human venture is based on the ability to communicate effectively. Every manager of business is compelled to motivate and communicate with mass communication which is the life line of business. In running any branch of business, thought is to be communicated clearly. Every piece of work in an office calls for some sort of communication of thought. The communication process is consistent in transmitting ideas, information and directing with a view to achieving a perfect identity of mind with another person. Breakdown of communication will produce misconception, unfavourable attitude, hostile situation and conflict of ideas and intentions.

Effective communication is the key to successful business. Starting from a trade enquiry of routine nature to the tendering of a detailed market report of a speech prepared by the chairperson of a company in a general body meeting–a good number of circumstances posing challenges are covered in the ambit of communication. Effective and efficient performance of work in any office calls for providing convenient and efficient means of communication. Provision of information with a sense of accuracy that too, when it is wanted most, will really help the management in performing the function effectively. Communication in a nutshell, is a *sine qua–non* for any kind of business.

Before we propose to understand the significance of communication from different angles, the following definitions authored by men of brilliance and excellence will certainly help us.

1. "Silence is golden"– lack of communication is a form of communication (Adage)

2. "Communication is the sum of all the things one person does when he wants to create an understanding in the mind of another. It is a bridge of meaning. It involves a systematic and continuous process of telling, listening and understanding". (Allen)

3. "In the context of a business enterprise, communication may be in the following forms:
   (a) An order (a managerial function of directing)
   (b) An appeal or a request (from workers to management)
   (c) An observation (a contributory to decision–making or one's own view)
   (d) An information (for general/statistical use of management)
   (e) An instruction (issued to subordinates as a part of delegation process)
   (f) In policy making (Whereby principle and standards are promulgated)" (Ronald R. Pit field–Bus orgn – 86.)

4. In the words of Comstock Glaser – "Such is the life of any executive reading or writing letters, memoranda, and reports constantly conferring and telephoning – such is a administration in general – a continuous round of written and verbal contact between workers and with outsiders".

5. "Communication is an exchange of facts, ideas, opinions or emotions by two or more persón" – (W.H. Newman and C.E. Summer, The Process of Management).

6. "The potentials of communication as a management tool are so great that it is difficult to recognise them, and easy to underrate them. Favourable dealings without side company contacts and effective relationships within an organisation depend upon communication."

7. It is the process of passing information and understanding from one person to another." – (Theo Haimann).

8. "Communication is the means by which the act of delegation is accomplished." – (Terry).

A perusal given to the above definitions makes one point clear that communication is the soul of management and has an all pervasive application in management. The most vital managerial tool is communication.

Significance of communication will be very well grasped only when we study under the following divisions. The subject of communication is so vast that it is difficult to summarise all of its divisions. Even then, a brief look of these is highly essential.

COMMUNICATION IN MANAGEMENT

(1) Goals (Objectives)	(2) Managerial Look	(3) Techniques Making	(4) Decision
(a) Clarity in expression (b) Two way communication (c) Training program (d) Information giving (e) Counselling (Advice) (f) Giving Direction (g) Acceptance trial of suggestions (h) Persuasion (i) Education (j) Giving caution Theory (k) Moral boosting (i) Prompting to work	(a) Management by objectives (1) Responsibility assignment (2) Job–Analysis (3) Present and future needs–assessment (4) Recruitment + selection (5) Personal Records + Appraisal (b) Supervision co-ordination + Delegation of Power (c) Graicunas	(1) Regular supervision (2) Personal contact (3) Use of telephone or telex (4) Use of common signs +posters (5) Grapevine (6) Agreement of opinion (consensus) (7) Pseudonymous letters*	(a) Upward communication (b) Downward flow (c) Measures + pre-requisites of above communication (d) Communication Log (e) Motivating employees (f) Safety + Discipline (g) Image building

5. Selection and Transmission of Message

(a) Clear goals (b) Careful assessment (c) Poor communication (d) Ridiculous +fatal (e) Response (f) Planning (g) No buck passing allowed.

6. Obstacles or Barriers to Communication

(a) Vague message (b) Editing Information (c) Loss in transmission and poor retention (d) in attention (e) Assumptions (f) Time factor (g) No confidence (h) Wrong judgement (i) Fear and failure (j) Noise, distance time, source, Jargon not understood (k) Semantics (slang with dual meanings)– Measures to improve communication.

7. Systematic Information – its criteria or principles

   (1) Unambiguity

   (2) No negligence

   (3) Loyalty

   (4) Informal sources–recognition

   (5) Implementation.

8. Vertical and Horizontal types of Communication

9. Problems of Communication

10. Written and Oral Communication
11. Committees and conferences – need advantages – Demerits Role of chairman and rules of meeting – Face to face meet – conduct of interviews – listening its significance.

All the points noted above under the heading communication in management should be understood in detail. Otherwise the proper role taken to by this part of managerial function will not be clear in our mind. Communication is an essential feature along with planning, organising, staffing, directing and controlling. Communication has a special function in directing.

Goal/Objectives in Communication

Communication is an inevitable human activity. To manage business affairs, exchange of ideas is a must. As in dumb and deaf society, communication can not be assumed to be lifeless and soundless. Area of marketing has its own codified language. One has to be aware of it.

(a) Clarity in expression: With the advance in all walks of life, special terms are coined to indicate certain position or ideas; it needs a good grasp of such an expression, conveyance should be smooth, clarity of ideas and precision in transmission of such ideas is a must. The common purpose of activity of any business should be properly understood; awareness of common goal is due to straight message.

(b) Two way communication: Every communication is a two way traffic. If cannot be one sided act. Ideas need a track to bring us intended reply. The type of response from receiver will very much depend upon how clearly the basic idea has been passed on from the original source.

(c) Training programme: Many organisations conduct this programme to impart training in their set purpose or aim for which they function. Goals, history, methods, participation, procedure involvement, clarifications, direction, rectification, achievements all need a variety of training schemes to be enlisted and chalked out for proper functioning of any set up.

(d) Information – giving: The basic objective of communication is to turn the static into dynamic. Pointless communication is a waste of time. Information to the given should be classified as basic and advance. It should be further labelled as simple and understandable, complex and technical. Organisational aims should reach the mass at large. It should not require further analysis and expertise for grasping. Nature of enquiry like price, channel selected like wholesale or retails mass addressed like private party, public or Govt., area chosen like agricultural, industrial, commercial, financial, technical etc., be pre–determined. Even the best possible brain may prove a failure in giving all possible information. But trails and errors are an accepted course. Scientific thinking and adoption of logical methods will help us a lot in this respect.

(e) Counselling (Advice): It means offering a better track of information with law, logic, prudence, wisdom and experience so that defect can be detected and rectified, and good results may be expected in the given situation.

(f) Giving direction: It means passing orders, showing the way and expecting a thing to be done in a desired manner. It should be sensible and possible. "Stop– buying those shares" "don't pay the cheque" "shift the premises" etc., should be circumstantially accepted. Obedience is a must. Establishing the authority of the communicator and replier is very essential.

(g) Acceptance and trial of suggestions: It means agreements with another to take cognizance of what he says for implementation. It also means readiness to carry out the expected job on the lines to improve the original idea. It also means readiness to do what is expected to be done, and also putting into action as a course of rectification and improvement of originally framed thought.

(h) Persuasion: Inducing, compelling, prompting a person to do or act, mostly in a positive way is persuasion. *Ex* : obtaining one's consent in execution of contract. Building up a circumstantial push to carry out a job.

(i) Giving caution: It refers to warnings. For example., "Trespassers will be prosecuted" "Don't exceed the dosage" "Halt and proceed" etc.

(j) Morale boosting: It refers to increasing the courage, confidence and capacity based on ethical aspects of one's life conditions; when conditions worsen, it gives a sense of right thinking. It empowers one's mind to remain calm and work minded. Failure is ignored and frustration will get dampened because of morale building, pushing, injecting and instilling capacity in men. Totally, it gives mental power to keep aside frustration and work hard, expecting good result.

(k) Prompting to work: It means supplying power to act. Creating a desire to work in a group coaxing, enticing, creating congenial atmosphere etc., comes within this ambit of motivation. Effective management needs communication which keeps men mentally rejuvenated to withstand stumblings and failings.

COMMUNICATION – ITS SCOPE

Communication has no boundary as such. Indoor information and message to the mass are two important wings or facts of the issue. Exercising control and building up of an image in the minds of public attached to the business are dominant factors, worker of production department, staff of administration, heads of the departments, the general manager, financial advisor, broker, consumer, auditor advertiser, researcher plant manager, banker all need different types of information concerning the organisation. Articles, memoranda, agenda, secretarial letters, announcements, speeches, code of conduct, corrigendum, memos, rules, regulations, writ petition, sales letter, explanations, deeds, representations, circulars, notices, reports–a wide range of information need to be considered under the caption of communication. Communication has much to do especially in the light of productivity based manager–worker–employee–public cordial relationship between management and employees has a greater impact on productivity. All this may be achieved by timely and sensible transmission of message i.e. communication.

Managerial Look at Communication

Management by Objectives : It is a scientific method and approach to Management. It includes fixation of objectives, control, review and development of management. It means action plan which includes (a) Development of "Responsibility fixation" (b) Managerial job analysis (c) Present and future needs (d) Recruitment and selection (e) Personal records and appraisal. Management by objectives or MBO implies responsibility establishment, structural improvement for management, profit centre identification, pinpointing talents and skills for promotion, improving the method of evaluation and knowing training needs. MBO has a feature of being applied perpetually. Achievements and failures must be examined after practising MBO. Purpose or targets should not be vague but verifiable. Staff cooperation is essential for its effective working. Participation of managers will help them in drafting meaning full derivative plans. Objectives with realistic basis need constructive participation and contribution. Time allowed, quantified targets and expected results are to be pre–determined. Monitoring the performance at various steps should be decided upon. Job details should be furnished and finalisation by an expert is needed.

Manager reviews the plans drawn by subordinates, offers suggestions and formal agreement is drawn up. Commitment for fulfillment is created. Skills and resources needed are considered. Challenge is faced with preparedness. Noting down of strong and weak points is required. Motivation, control and prediction of result are made possible. Horizontal method of co–ordination is desirable. Mutual understanding and respect will help the task of co–ordination and communication very much. Inter–change of information which will help in solving problems may be anticipated and solved due to continuous communication. Structure of organisation and personal skill will help in producing effective communication. Memos, bulletins and wireless along with letters supplement personal contact. Improper and defective communication methods may cause perplexity, bewilderment, waste of time, loss of property and danger to life.

Graicunas Theory

It shows the possible relationships between a manager and his subordinates when subordinates are a good number. Personal attention with lot of frequency and time involved will go theoretical possible and constant communication between among a supervisor and two or more subordinates may be considered as follows :

(1) A to B
(2) A to C
(3) B to A
(4) C to A
(5) B to C
(6) A to B and C

Frustration and loss of managerial efficiency will be seen.

When rungs of the ladder are many, subordinates will feel isolated from top management. Plans and policies will not be fully grasped. Communication gap will be widened. Self–reliance and initiative will vanish.

Techniques in Communication

Techniques means method of performance and manipulation especially with everything concerned with mechanical part of artistic performance. It influences management span and also communication impact. Good objective standards and personal supervision will reveal deviations and reduce waste of time. Key subordinates should be entrusted with the job of top manager to communicate on his behalf. To avoid vagueness and misunderstanding and to get instruction, advice or clarification, written chits may be encouraged. Strict protocol of the chain of command or through proper channel should be set aside. Examples of technique of modern communication include buzzer, telephone, internal telephone, dictating machine, walkie talkie, electronic device etc.

Telephone

Advantages

(1) It is a vital tool of communication of present society.

(2) It has advantage of quickness.

(3) It saves time and money.

(4) It is a cheap mode of communication.

Disadvantages

(1) Several lines are needed for large organisation.

(2) Service may be inefficient.

(3) Quite often it may go out of order.

(4) Clear hearing may be difficult in longer distance talk.

(5) Always speakers and listeners must be alert.

Telex

It consists of an automatic electric typewriter and a dial box. There is a telex directory. Each station has a code number. It provides automatic communication through the printed words between subscribers in cities with telex exchanges. Charges for a telex call start as soon as the number is connected. It runs very fast. Drawbacks include bad wording of message inadequacy, of course, it is the fastest and efficient communication system.

Signs and Posters

These are the best methods of communication. For conveying the public message, it is quite effective *Ex:* "School Zone", "go slow", "silence please", "Curve Ahead", "Push", "Pull", "Danger 400 Volts", "No Admission" "No parking", "No right Turn", "No posters here" etc.

Silence

It is more effective than fluent speech. Short pause emphasises much, it makes audience alert. It does not mean total stop for speech but a suspension of speech. Silence may be said to be dead, stony or embarrassing. It may indicate absence of thought or fullness of feelings, anger or displeasure. In fact facial expression, posture or movement may denote feeling behind silence In public speech, silence is more effective than table thumping. In times of human anguish wrath, suffering, sympathy, condolence or overwhelming joy silence is prominent form of communication. Silence has legal sanctity and is declared not a fraud by Section 17 of Contract Act of 1872. Section 143 of the same Act declares that guarantee obtained by creditor by being silent is invalid. Silence can be awkward also as it creates a gap in communication Depending upon person and situation silence may be harmful also. Irrespective of positive or negative outcome of silence it should be given a recognition as being a method of communication.

Grapevine

It means and refers to rumour and gossip regarding policies and plans of management. It is an informal communication method or pattern. It is a secondary personal channel. It has no direction. It is largely horizontal. It is oral information woven and flown. It may move along in a chain from person to person.

Source of information is a talk between men at meal tables due to close contract in travelling together, as men of similar temperaments. Matters of mutual talk may be individual manager, work programmes, corporate performance, policy matters, disciplinary action, theft, fire, dividend, character and conduct, immoral happenings, behaviour etc. Bias, jealousy, prejudice, malafide intentions will be a colouring reason of what might be talked over. Episodes may be an influential one. Harmful lie begins to travel fast and faster than the truth. It has no problem of delay in delivery of message. Opinions, beliefs, attitudes, willingness, excitement and bad temper will kill the efficiency. The baseless bulletins normally mar the relationships and productivity of the concern. Bad news and unpleasant stories run at a galloping rate. Management has to take quick action to nip in the bud. Management may speak out the truth through notice boards and distributions of bulletins. Places and timings for grapevine are coffee–break, toilet, canteen, notice–Board, drinking water–place. Examples of gossip information are (1) Did Manager come back from official tour? (2) Staff–bonus how much this year? (3) Stopping free coffee supply? (4) Retrenchment of an employee (5) Is foreign contract over? (6) Success of union in matters before tribunal etc.

Grapevine satisfies gregarious instincts of man, management should cautiously utilise grapevine channel to motivate men and improve their moral.

Opinion–agreement (Consensus)

It refers to common agreement on set purpose. Open contest, protest, rebut, challenge and opposition may be zeroed by obtaining consensus of the concerned. In amicable and homogenous meetings and conferences, this method is followed. Faith, zeal and skill of the manager and mass is a must for this type of communication–adoption.

Pseudonymous Letters

These are nameless and without signature–Names, if indicated, will be untrue. Individual writer/s identity is concealed. In the letters addressed to the press, names may be atleast, revealed to the editor. These are called anonymous letters found in correspondence with law enforcing authorities, regarding shirking of responsibility, avoidance of tax–payment, evasion of customs duty to government etc. To eliminate nuisance of oppression caused by gamblers, drunkards and thieves, crime–detection etc., this gives valuable information. It throws light on corruption, bribery, thief–searching etc. Though it is legally not supportable, it is still useful in certain cases as detailed above.

COMMUNICATION AND DECISION–MAKING

Everyone is an originator of information in any organisation. Both the supervisor and the employees are equally responsible. Important factors to be considered here are – (a) Time (b) Matter (c) Addressee (d) Oral/ written (e) Techniques (f) Formal channels and (g) Informal channels.

Business manager's office is always flooded with information. Information desirable may not be available. Very important items of information may not be forthcoming. Many a time the quantum and dependability will have to be examined before acceptance. Delay, failure, labour, cost, consistency, relevance and utility of information received should be consciously verified for future decisions.

Upward Flow

It starts from supervisor level. It goes to departmental manager who will send it to the general manager for his decision. Selection and assessment will be manager's task. It can be verified from different sources like friends, clubs, market, other organisations, private detectives, spies etc., good and positive relationship among members of the organisation is the only way to bring about improvement in the upward flow of information.

Objective of Upward Communication

This includes (a) Periodical reporting (b) Information from newspaper, magazines, journals, gazettes and articles (c) Requests of staff for favour or permission (d) Application for leave or job. (e) Individual or collective appeals (f) Union–demands (g) Representations for promotion (h) Complaints for faults and defects in the system (i) Suggestions for changes, improvements, psycho-desires, for rules, for quality upgradation, service–conditions, public relations, cost reduction, accidents–avoidance, profit raising etc.

Suggestions help us in getting bright ideas. Employees feel that they can make healthy contribution, their grievances can be redressed.

Downward Flow

It moves downward from supervisors to subordinates at different levels of the organisation. Through this flow, management plans, decisions and directives are communicated to lower levels for implementation.

Downward information includes, instruction for job performance, creating an understanding, informing rules, regulations, policies, procedures, practices, feed back to the subordinate about job–performance, creating a sense of belonging to the concern and job–commitment.

Objectives of Downward Communication Include

Information–provision, Instruction, Order, Request, Advice, Counselling, Training, Warning, Notice, Appreciation, Motivation, Persuasion, Morale raising etc.

Communication Log

It means record of formal and official communications carefully made concerning office registers, head office, officers, managers, their daily work, oral communications, if any.

It is a daily record made in the chronological order. It includes letter writing, reports, memos, phone calls, visitors–remarks, meeting, speech, lecture interviews, factory visits and inspection. It helps in economy of time.

Motivating Employees

Communication is inevitable here. A sense of belonging to the organisation is always necessary. Employer must care for their safety and security. Communication is the medium for this. Communication begins with the appointment of an employee. Factory address, products produced, services rendered, credit worthiness, capital investment information etc., should be supplied to the workers to create a feeling towards the concern. Workers should know the procedure, practice, services and facilities of the organisation in the light of its philosophy. Information, supervision, freedom of action, fearless operational devotion, zeal, responsible attitude and team spirit will be possible only through proper appraisal of the position Objective analysis, observation, judgement, periodical survey, detection of errors and deviations, morale–improvements will certainly enhance the efficiency and help in goal–achievement. Enforcement of safety measures requires efficient communication.

Image–building

Educational institutes, clinics, hospitals, trade organisations, business concerns, corporate bodies, banks, manufactures–all stand in the queue to earn their reputation in society. Document of every one of these bodies would try to contain their history of formation and working to catch the eye of needy mass. Indispensability of their services will be broadcast only through clear, convincing and careful structure of message. Name and fame of any business entity can be earned only by well worded and competent communication system.

Selection and Transmission of Message

This shows readiness for communicating. Information is obtained from divergent sources. No information is available in a source at once. Hence, careful selection of what kind of information is wanted, what is available? should be analysed. Awkward situations may emerge due to faulty and wrong information–collection. Owing to unreliable information, heavy expense may be incurred. Sometimes, it proves fatal. Therefore, careful planning to collect, to analyse, to clarify, to codify, and to communicate is highly essential. Absence of planning will mean "duty of all is duty of none". Avoiding, evading, shrinking, lurking, bypassing, misconveying, pretending, tale telling, discarding, disowning of duties and responsibilities or buck passing can be totally avoided, if clear cut message is previously made available to all the levels of authorities in the business concern. Definiteness of source, unbiased selection and fearless data provision will mean effective communication.

Obstacles or Barriers to Communication

Intention of message giver is not easy to communicate because there are innumerable difficulties and problems. These are called barriers to communication. The chief aim of the communication is to get a definite response. Barriers may be defective mechanical device, human attitude or bad language. Communication becomes complete and purposeful only when the informer and the informed evince keen interest in the transmission and reception of ideas. Communication has no terminus but it is circutous. Complete organisational structure influences communication. Environment contributes to its success. Good communication net work should be there. Information furnishing for decision making and tuning the workers demeanour to meet the needs of organisation should be the goal of any concern. Manager and employee should have cordial relationship for purposeful communication.

Now, let us know in some detail the barriers to communication noted in the list given below:

(a) Vague Message: Message should be perfect and unambiguous. Bad expression should be avoided. It should not be inappropriate, indefinite and incomplete. Impertinent matter should be left out. Unclear or indefinite message needs correction. Both time and money will go waste. Hence, clarity in communication is to be insisted upon.

(b) Editing Information: No information can be repeated without omission, understandable language should be used. Improper translation will mean inefficiency in communication.

(c) Loss in Transmission and Poor Retention: All that is told gets lost in course of passing it on to a number of people. Poor memory of majority of listeners is one such reason. Reminders, repetitions and clarifications are a normal course of action due to poor human retention power.

(d) Inattention: Carelessness, inadvertence, irresponsibility, lack of interest in listening to always result in this.

(e) Assumptions: Vague delegation of authority will give rise to piling up of files. Uncertain messages will cause delay. Clear ambit for discharge of duties and clear cut authority will help clear off the files. *Ex:* "for needful", "for perusal", "for anticipated" will be deemed obstacles to communication.

(f) Time–Factor: Important communication on matters relating to shifting of business premises, layoff, retrenchment, power of attorney, bonus–declaration, overtime order, etc. should be soon brought to the notice of all the employees. Sensitive issues should be well worded and warded off.

(g) No Confidence: Before drafting any letter dealing with outside it should be a well settled matter. Intermittent letters with negation and approval will be loosely viewed, This irresponsibility will affect communication very much. For purposeful communication, the receiver of information should not have any distrust in the communicator.

(h) Wrong Judgement: To form an opinion, to pass a judgement or to give a reply, premature assessment is to be discouraged. In hearing, recording, reading or communicating, the entire message is to be allowed to be transmitted. Any decision on half heard issue will damage the system/ person/entity/position as the case may be.

(i) Fear and Failure: Intentional incomplete information or withholding the message or partial information may be due to fear attributable to inferiority or anticipation of irksomeness, awkwardness, keeping ones' self aloof, wash off hands, to be fishy etc.

Laziness, lack of motivation, feeling shy of, prejudice, bequeathed serfdom will result in interruption to free flow of communication.

(j) Noise, distance, time, source, jargon not understood: Personal talk is the best. Delayed and untimely message will be of no avail to the recipient of it. Some sources of information may not have public honour. Message, even if right and true, may be disbelieved by the majority. Gauging of such message will certainly distort it. Unheard, half recorded or off the records cannot serve a reliable passage of message. Moreover, specially coined bazar words will not be easily understood by many. The result of using high sounding words is only confusion and improper communication.

(k) Semantics: It means the science of the development of words. Vulgar words with dual meanings should be removed from respectful messages. It results in faulty communication, if slang is used. Vulgar vocabulary is always vulnerable, and not venerable in cultured communication. For example: chair, pig, present, cite, site, red–carpet, vice, etc.

Measures to Improve Communication

1. Manager should grow responsible and trustworthy.
2. Hospitable environment should be created.
3. Freedom of expression should not be unnecessarily curtailed.
4. It should be a two way traffic.
5. Mutual understanding and cordiality should be supported.
6. Oral message should be validated.
7. Rumours/ gossips/ tell–a–tale/ sychophancy/ use of slang/ mutual disrespect words etc. should be totally avoided.
8. Sufficient allocation of finances in the budget should be made.

All these will obviate the difficulties and improve the communication system as such.

SYSTEMATIC INFORMATION – ITS CRITERIA OR PRINCIPLES

Owing to variable factors like human thought, attitude, decision, behaviour etc. perfection in communication is many a time an illusion. Demarcation and delivery of message should be considered with a sense of accuracy and relevance. Depending upon the quality of information , the position of receiver, method of passing on the message and mechanical channel employed following broad principles may be recommended:

1. Unambiguity: It means clarity of information. Jargon should be avoided. Common expression is to be used. The idea of the sender of information should be faithfully and truly transmitted to the receiver.

2. No Negligence: All messages should be received with full attention. Concentration is very essential. Manipulation of message is to be fully discouraged. Extension of human minimum courtesy is hearing and recording is equally essential. Lethargy and repugnance should have no place in transmission of messages.

3. Loyalty: It means integrity. A sense of being sincere to the concern with regularity and faith is labelled as loyally. Conscious effort is needed. Different stages of authority should be respected. In case of need, irrespective of flow, work should be done in the larger interests of the concern. No one should betray the organisational interests but enrich it with regularity and good result–oriented approach.

4. Informal Sources–Recognition: In several organisations, many live on information obtained from higher sources on private occasions. They have both constructive and destructive impacts. *Ex:* (1) overhearing the statement of top officers at a private gathering and setting afloat the news. (2) Management may use tactics to curb the prominence of union leaders who might be incorrigible and lawful (3) Taking undue advantage of opinion poll for promotion by being secret releaser to popularise himself and to gain a whip thereby, in subordinate circle.

5. Implementation: (1) Constant training (2) Timely reacting to the message (3) Awareness regarding objectives will undoubtedly help in the implementation of change in the area of communication. No single individual can aim at this. It should be a collective programme with a sense of determination to inject necessary changes in the minds of all especially in a complex organisation.

Thus, principles of effective communication are summed up as follows.

1. Use of simple and understandable language.
2. Selection of right medium of communication.
3. Clarity of message is essential.
4. Creation of cordial atmosphere.
5. Sufficiency of information.
6. Training to the communicators.
7. Staff co–operation and co–ordination.
8. Follow–up action to know the result.
9. Effective listening.
10. Consistent communication and
11. Timeliness of communication.

VERTICAL AND HORIZONTAL TYPES OF COMMUNICATION

1. Vertical Communication: It refers to communication between management and subordinates. It is called inter–scalar or two way communication. It is formal communication. It may be downward or upward communication already discussed in previous pages.

2. Horizontal Communication: It is that which flows between persons of equal status in an organisation. It may be oral or written. Exchange of mutual information between two or more departments is the purpose behind it. It is more at higher authority levels. Higher level officers like departmental managers will have constant consultation, whereas two clerks of two different departments may not be close.

Features of communication are as follows:

1. It is a two way traffic between Sender and Receiver.
2. It presupposes existence of facts, information, opinion, emotion, suggestions or ideas to be passed on.
3. Two basic channels are formal and informal.
4. Important communication are words, pictures and action.
5. It travels up and down and side to side.
6. It provides a link between organisation and outside agencies.

The most common barriers to communication may be summed up as follows:

1. Complex organisation structure.
2. Formal and rigid relationships.
3. Semantic barriers.
4. Poorly constructed communication.
5. Failure of the medium used.
6. Volume of communication.
7. Behavioural barriers.
8. Other barriers include inadequate staff, faulty procedures, inaccuracy in processing and delivery of communication, loss of documents and files, failure of the staff to follow the procedure laid down etc.

Problems of communication are the following:

1. Distortion due to noise and ambiguous words used in the message.
2. Filtering meaning 'alternation or twisting out of context the message'.
3. Channels are over loaded. Relevant, routine, urgent and vital cannot be easily separated.
4. Simultaneous release of several messages, difficulty in segregation and transmission.
5. Problem of identifying organisational structure and routing the correspondence.
6. Assumption that both communicator and communicatee are of the same mind, attitude, temperament etc.
7. Mass communication received maddens the manager.
8. Separating useful from useless information needs faculty of selection.

9. Communication involves, wastages, irrelevance, duplication, overlapping, stationery, stamps and high cost.
10. Decision to be taken regarding Integrated Data Processing (I.D.P.) or Electronic Data Processing (E.D.P.)

Written Communication

It includes letters, memos, orders, instructions, reports, returns and bulletins securing as the basis of communication.

Advantages:

(a) Legal records for disputes and for further reference.

(b) They have widest coverage.

(c) Personal presence of both not required at all at any place.

Disadvantages:

(a) More of stationery, hence expensive.

(b) Improper language, may hurt the feelings.

(c) It is time–consuming and costly.

Oral Communication

It is in the form of spoken word, it may be face to face or through telephone or other device.

Advantages:

(a) Ideal for confidential matters.

(b) Cordial personal exchange of ideas is possible.

(c) Speedy interchange of ideas is feasible.

Disadvantages:

(a) Ineffective for lengthy communication.

(b) No contractual records available.

(c) Vocal expression may be easily mis–understood.

Means of Written Communication are: (a) Agenda forms (b) Annual Reports (c) Bulletins (d) Correspondences (e) House journals and Magazines (f) Memoranda (g) Minutes (h) Official publication (i) Organisation Manuals (j) Organisation schedules (k) Policy manuals (l) Procedure manuals (m) Teleprinters (n) Trade journals (o) Suggestion schemes etc.,

Oral Communications include: (a) Course for trainees (b) Interviewing (c) Joint consultation (d) Meeting and conferences (e) Personnel Department (f) Radio (g) Telephone system (h) Television (i) Sales representation (j) Trade unions etc.,

Note: PAX= Private Automatic Exchange

PABX= Private Automatic Branch Exchange

Intercom= Automatic system of office intercommunication

PX= Private Exchange

PBX= Private Branch Exchange

PCO= Public Call Office

SFT= Subscription Fixed Time

F.T.C= Fixed Time Calls

Internal Communication

It is also known as intercommunication. It refers to the transmission or exchange of thought and messages between persons and departments of the same organisation.

External Communication

It involves exchange of messages with outsiders.

Listening

It means not only hearing but also to get the full meaning of what is said and heard. Both the speaker and the listener have to encode and decode the information. As per research, listening takes away about 45%, while speaking 30%, reading 16%, and writing 9%. Executives should be trained in listening. Listener should particularly take note of words chosen by the speaker, his emotion, his exaggeration, anger, insult, satire, negligence, tone, gesture and keeping mum. Retention, rectification and efficiency differ between two listeners.

Significance of Hearing

To be attentive speaks of 'one's culture'. Listening in a way is indicative of one's tranquil state of mind. Decision–making needs a lot of listening to men of information. It grades human relations by increasing respect for supervisor's job. Worker's grievances can be readdressed by showing sympathy in hearing them. Liberty to speak will extend a chance to the employee to show his attachment to work, zeal and responsibility. Good listening avoids waste of time and energy. Good listening reduces verbal conflict and prevents tempers from flying at meetings and conferences. For effective execution of job assigned, proper listening is equally significant. It improves conversational skill. The power of an individual to be highly attentive, receptive, active and responsive is very much revealed in listening to music, poetry, drama, recitation, talk, speech, elocution contest, etc.,

Listening– a Disciplined Behaviour

It is neither a negative behaviour nor is a passive one but, a positive mental function.

Factors which prevent you from being a good listener are:

(a) Noise, human disturbance and telephone;

(b) Preoccupation of listener's mind or physical pain like headache;

(c) Speakers lacking in clarity and too much of speed. Average speaking speed is 120–130 words a minute; brain's receiving speed is three times more;

(d) Preparing one's self for interrogation;

(e) Dullness, boredom and lack of interest;

(f) Avoiding to hear talk on important and difficult topic;

(g) Inclination to afford criticism on speaker's style, voice etc. than the matter;

(h) Incapacity to jot down due to difference in speech, hearing retaining, assessing, summarising and writing down;

(i) Not coming out of traditional methods hence, modern thinking is neglected;

(j) Speech needs a contextual consideration rather than 'go by lexicon'; and

(k) Other factors of good listening include facial expression, excitement, omission of other facts and figures etc.

Rules of good listening are:

(1) Stop talking;

(2) Give freedom to speaker;

(3) Show a desire to listen to and pay serious attention to;

(4) Avoid distraction, disturbance, interruption and irritation to the speaker;

(5) Have full patience and let the speaker know it;

(6) Place yourself in speaker's position (Empathy);

(7) Don't pass judgement, don't have bias against the speaker but, fully hear him;

(8) Frame only pertinent questions after your efforts to understand him; and

(9) Shut up your mouth and let your mind work, then draw conclusions on "speech and hearing".

Factors to be considered as effective means of communication are:

(1) Distance (2) Accuracy (3) Secrecy (4) Certainty (5) Speed (6) Safety (7) Read (8) Impression (9) Cost (10) Need for trained staff and (11) Convenience in use.

Question of one's convenience as officer, manager should be considered in detail before he decides upon which are the other factors to be taken note of. Any hasty decision will mean waste of time. Sometimes, the quickest and safest mode of communication has to be relied upon. Much risk of tension can be dispensed with, if only the above factors are kept in mind.

Committees and Conferences

These are called "group process" or "group communication". Business functioning has become complex. These committees and conferences provide a chance to share common interests and problems. Members with varied and enviable designations and dexterity will be invited to participate in decision making process. Group discussion provides : (a) understanding a situation (b)possibility–exploration and (c) solving problems. A group discussion allows for the expression of a variety of viewpoints. It gives a sense of participation in the discussion. Decision through discussion is more acceptable than the decision imposed from above. Both are expensive and time consuming. Arrangements and travel will be a big problem. Purposeful participation is always profitable. Committee is a managerial tool, whereas conference is a learning and training ground. Committee is time and task bound whereas conference is free to recommend. A committee meets at intervals and has a long existence whereas, a conference is a series of meetings and may be held for 2 or 3 days. A committee is appointed with authority whereas a conference is held for discussion, training exchanging views, experience and opinions. According to L. Hall "A committee is a person or body of persons to which a specific duty (or duties) has been delegated. It is, therefore, a form of delegation".

Examples of committees are : Management, Audit, Bonus, Policy, Wage and Salary, Revenue, Grievances, Discipline, Welfare etc.

Kinds of Committee include:

(a) Executives committee (Management committee– with authority)

(b) Standing committee (Transfer/ Finance/ Allotment)

(c) Adhoc committee (Investigation or Advice on schemes) (Fact finding/ special)

(d) Sub–committee (Routine or specific enquiry)

(e) Joint committee (Employer– employees committee).

Conferences: According to L.Hall, "A conference, like any form of joint consultation, is primarily an occasion for two–way communication. It is, however, frequently used as a means of communicating policy".

Advantages of Committee are:

(a) Specilised knowledge can be applied

(b) Duties of direction can be distributed

(c) Business can be considered in greater detail

(d) Fewer full board meetings are required and

(e) More time is available.

Disadvantages of Committee are:

(a) Authority of Board may be weakened

(b) Delays may occur

(c) Weak management may hide behind a committee and

(d) A committee often tends to be dominated by an over–bearing member.

Responsibilities of Participants in the Conferences are:

(a) A good sporting spirit

(b) Graciousness to compliment others for good point/ remark

(c) Supporting harmonious meeting to be conducted

(d) Avoiding anger, jealousy, revenge, spite, emotion etc.

(e) Willing co–operation and polite presentations.

(f) Unbiased hearing and patience to capture other's views and opinions

(g) Active participation with regularity to gather ideas and excellence of others and

(h) Wholehearted co–operation to the success of the conference.

Correspondence and Mail Service

Correspondence is communication with outsiders by letters, with a view to building up business. Reputation depends upon, (a) Quality of letters and (b) Method of correspondence. Effective organisation of correspondence department is essential to successful business.

Written communication through the post office or messenger service is generally described as "Mail". Business mail may be classified into: (1) Inwards or Incoming Mail, (2) Outwards or Outgoing Mail, and (3) Interdepartmental Mail. These 3 classes of mail may consist of letters, circulars, telegrams, remittances etc.

Correspondence work is entrusted to a component officer who may be the secretary. The department is divided into two branches– one for handling inward correspondence and other for expediting, the drafting and despatch of letters addressed to outsiders.

'Inward Correspondence' in the words of Thomas Evelyn, "the organisation of Inward Correspondence is very important, for on this depend the prompt despatch of orders, the safe handling of remittances, adequate attention to complaints, and in general smooth running of the business as a whole".

Incoming letters may pertain to offers, quotations, invoices, orders, remittances, complaints, directions and cancellations, representation etc.

Inward Mail Routine (Incoming Mail)

(a) Opening all letters under supervision sometime before office opens;

(b) Classifying covers unopened as

(i) Private (General executive)

(ii) Confidential (official) and

(iii) Special;

(c) Checking empty and remaining envelopes;

(d) Passing on the contents to the supervisor for examination and recording of remittances;

(e) Stamping cheques, entering in a book and passing it on to the cashier;

(f) Stamping on all letters with date and time;

(g) Sorting out letters and placing in different trays;

(h) Handing over all letters to different departments by a literate attender;

(i) Supervision will be left with undelivered letters, parcels and telegrams for necessary action.

Outward Correspondence

It is vital matter. Letters should be drafted with impressive and courteous character and style. Object should be (a) Business expansion and (b) Good will creation. Clerical rough drafts should be fully read, verified and corrected before final letters are typed out or hand written by the staff incharge. Full text and enclosures if any, should be approved and confirmed. These should be clear and action/ purpose oriented. Outgoing letters are often construed as ambassadors carrying message, emblem, responsibility and respect of the business organisation concerned.

Outward Mail Routine (Outgoing Mail Or Despatch)

'Despatching' literally means 'Sending off the mail' i.e., putting the mail in course of transmission either through a messenger or delivering it to the nearest post or telegraph office.

Outward Mail Routine

(a) Folding of letters and inserting them into envelopes;

(b) Sealing and stamping;

(c) Entering in outward Mail Register or Post Book;

(d) Posting or delivery of the Mail.

Despatch clerk or Secretary will do the above work in a small business but in a large establishment, there may be a different section or department or executing this job. This is considered as the core of office–routine.

STUDY QUESTIONS

Section A

(2 Marks Questions - Answer in 4 lines each)

1. Give the meaning of Business Communication?
2. What is Correspondence in Business?
3. Is Conversation better form than written communication?
4. Mention any four mechanical devices that help us transmit messages.
5. What do you mean by stereotyped phrase? Do you still use it?
6. Define Jargon? Give two examples of it?
7. Mention the features of clear writing.
8. Define "Communication".
9. Mention any four objectives of communication.
10. What do you mean by 'clarity in expression'?
11. What do you mean by 'Training Programme'?
12. What do you mean by Counselling?
13. Does Communication boost Morale?
14. Give any four examples of technique of communication?
15. Mention two advantages and two disadvantages of Telephone.
16. What do you mean by Telex?
17. Give four examples of signs and posters.
18. Is silence a means of communication?
19. What do you mean by "grape vine'?
20. What do you know about pseudonymous letters?
21. Mention reasons for upward communication.
22. Mention four objectives of downward communication.
23. What is "Communication Log'?
24. Mention any 4 barriers of communication.

25. What do you mean by SEMANTICS?
26. Mention any four measures to improve communication.
27. Mention any 4 principles of communication.
28. What is Vertical Communication?
29. What is Horizontal Communication?
30. Mention any 4 problems of communication?
31. What does written communication include?
32. What do you mean by 'Oral communication'?
33. Mention any 2 advantages of "oral communication'?
34. Mention any 4 features of communication?
35. Mention any 4 means of Written Communication?
36. What does oral communication include?
37. What is internal communication?
38. What is external communication?
39. What do you mean by 'listening to' in communication?
40. Mention any 4 factors which prevents you from listening?
41. Mention any 4 rules of good listening.
42. Mention any 4 factors considered for effective means of communication.
43. What does Committee do as a means of communication?
44. What do 'Conferences' mean in the area of communication?
45. Is 'Correspondence' different from communication?
46. What do you mean by 'Mail'? Mention its divisions.
47. What do 'Inward' and 'Outward' correspondence mean?
48. What is "Inwards Mail routine'?
49. What is "Outward Mail routine'?
50. Give 4 examples of how orders are conveyed between two countries?

Section B

(8 Marks Questions - Answer in 30 lines each)

1. Briefly explain how communication would evolve itself in human society?
2. "Precision and quickness' are the key words for successful communication. Do you agree?
3. Does 'Correspondence' mean 'Communication'?

4. Account for the contributions of modern mechanical aids to improve 'Communication'.
5. "Lucidity means rapidity Communication". Explain.
6. "Verbosity means ambiguity in communication". Explain.
7. "Prolonged passage conveys no meaningful message". Explain.
8. "Effective correspondence will add to the beauty of Business entity". Explain.
9. "Goals of communication will help us determine the media in communication". How?
10. "Communication has no boundary as such". Explain.
11. What areas does communication cover?
12. Explain the scope of communication?
13. Bring out the significance of communication.
14. Explain Graicunas theory in Managerial communication.
15. Explain the techniques of communication.
16. What is "the place of silence" as a means of communication?
17. Explain grapevine with reference to its (a) Sources and (b) Gossip information.
18. What role does communication play in decision making in a Business set up?
19. Explain upward communication.
20. Explain downward communication.
21. How does communication help in enforcement of safety and discipline?
22. Is communication a competent weapon in Business image building?
23. What is selection and transmission of message?
24. Explain Barriers to communication with reference to vagueness and inattention.
25. How do editing and loss in Transmission account for being barriers to communication?
26. Do Time factor, Assumption, No confidence create barrier to communication?
27. In what way do noise, fear and failure plus wrong judgement become obstacles to communication?
28. What is Semantics? State the measures to improve communication.
29. Explain "Unambiguity' and 'Loyalty' as principles of communication.
30. Do you accept "No negligence' and " recognition of informal sources' as criteria of communication?
31. Briefly explain all the principles of effective communication.
32. What are 'Vertical' and 'Horizontal' communication methods?
33. What are the features of effective communication.?

34. Explain the problems of communication.

35. Enlist different communication problems.

36. State the merits and demerits of oral communication.

37. What is written communication? Mention its advantages and disadvantages.

38. Expand the following abbreviations and write a very brief note on each of them:

    (a) PAX (b) PABX

    (c) Intercom (d) PX

    (e) PBX (f) PCO

    (g) SFT and (h) F.T.C

39. Is 'listening' necessary to accomplish listening in communication in business.

40. Explain the importance of listening the objective of communication?

41. State the rules of good listening.

42. Mention the factors which prevent you from being a good listener.

43. Account for committees and conference in Business– communication.

44. State the responsibilities of participants in conferences relating to Business.

45. Explain correspondence and mail service.

46 . Give a brief account of inward mail routine.

47. Give a brief account of outward mail routine.

48. What do you mean by "Inward" and "Outward" mails routines?

Section C

(15 Marks Questions - Answer in 3 pages each)

1. What is the place of communication in human society?

2. Is communication indispensable to Business?

3. Comment on the view that an inappropriate choice of the medium of communication leads to communication failure.

4. Write brief notes on Silence, Facial expression and gestures as accompaniments of oral communication.

5. Explain (a) Consensus (b) Grapevine and (c) communication Log.

6. Write short notes on communication:

    (a) For counselling

    (b) For motivation and

    (c) For raising morale.

7. Explain barriers to communication.
8. Distinguish between Committee and Conference.
9. Does communication demand or command managerial look in Business arena?
10. Explain Nature, Importance and Scope of Business Communication.

*****

CHAPTER 2

STRUCTURE OF BUSINESS LETTERS

- Definition
- Illustrative Indentions
- Full Block Form
- Essentials of a Good Business Letter

Structure means arrangement of parts. Elements of a business letter should be properly arranged. It is the physical appearance of a letter. The letter is analogous to salesman. It is representative of its sender. Improper and unpleasant look fails to capture the attention of its reader. Reader's opinion on sender will be very much dependent on how it looks before it is read. Letter-writing is an art. One should cultivate this art of writing letters. Business letters are to a larger extent formal when compared to the letters between friends. Quite often the forms of letters are the outcome of experience and custom. A salesman with pleasing personality, with a fine suit, with seasoned demeanour, in fine speech with a sense of self dignity and mutual respect will bring the business the name and fame. In the same way, a business letter demands of us, a decent dress and a neat look with reasonable parts. These parts with a logical sequence will add to the beauty of letter "frame-work". The traditions of trade have already set out the forms in consonance with occasions. Even then, the factors like, relevance, look, dignity, space, time, clarity, brevity etc., should be aptly used.

Physical appearance of a business letter has a purpose of providing a good get up. It attracts his attention. It is like an attractive dress of a person.

Physical appearance means and includes (a) Qualitative stationery used (b) Typing without errors (c) Clear conveyance of information in several paragraphs called "Spacing" (d) Paper-colour used with envelopes (e) Use of neatly cut sheets duly numbered (f) Name of the writer and his address (letterhead).

- **What paper to use:** Cheap, oily, torn-out, mutilated and glossy paper should not be used for letter-writing. Good quality paper should be used.
- **Size:** Standard sheet measuring 8½" by 11" is normally found in practice. Use of a quarter sheet will not create a good impression of the writer. It shows niggardly character of the writer.
- **Quality indicates:** (1) no blurring (2) no blotting (3) no delicacy and tearing in nature (4) firm texture white paper (5) it withstands rough handling (6) 20 lbs paper is suitable (7) good bond or linen paper is preferable (8) it is fit for piercing through the rod for filing purpose.

Fast colours should be discouraged and preferably white and snow-white be recommended. Heavy red, deep yellow, dark green, twinkling blue must not be much desired. In fact, except for white paper, preference of top colours should be discouraged. If at all coloured paper is to be used, for segregating the items manufactured, careful planning is needed.

- **Letterheads contain details to** indicate the name, telegraph, telephone, telex, cable, etc. It should be as far as possible brief. Simple letterhead creates dignity and avoids company intention printing of superior officers' names and their addresses, telephone numbers, telegraphic details and exhibition of trade mark if any should be avoided.

- **Typing:** Hand-written letters are deemed quite out-dated now. It is laborious and difficult to manage. All writing may not be readable. Some of them may be a scribble or a scrawl. Neatly typed out letters will make reading easy. Typing has out-beaten the hand-written letters owing to the advantages of xerox and preservation of the copies in concerned files. Double spacing is desirable, if the letter matter is not much. Single spacing is sufficient if it is a long letter; in such a case double spacing looks pleasing between paragraphs. Any hasty and erratic typing will spoil the beauty and dignity of such a letter. Hence, a lot of care is to be taken to avoid mis–spelling of words and heavily impressed erasures. Godrej or Remington typing machines with name and fame of their own will ensure us of quality in impression of alphabets and mechanical case in handling. Even if xerox is desired, it demands of us a well typed out letter flawless in words and mechanics. Today most of the offices use computers.

- **Folding:** Neat folding of letter is partly the result of decency and artistic ability. Careful folding of a letter, that too with enclosures needs a continuous and cautious work. Inadvertent folding will create crease and smash the very look of it, when it is opened for reading. Floppish appearance of fastidious typed letter will be fully spoilt, if crease is observed in elite correspondence. The procedure of folding is a matter of convenience. Size of the paper used will count here. In case window-envelope is used, inside address should be made to be transparent through the tissue paper.

- **Envelope:** Eye-catching but still, matching colour-paper should be used. Envelope and letterhead paper quality should be identical. Parrot green, skyblue, rose like and pink are much desired. Pink is preferred quite often by many in business world. If enclosures are more, window envelopes may be avoided .Even when matters of utmost confidence are to be dealt with persons, window envelope's may be dispensed with. Normally, sender's address must find its place in the upper left hand corner of the front. The "to address" should also be unerratic in typing it out.

Business Letter - Its Display and Sketch

Logical placement of information refers to arrangement and the decent look refers to 'letter appearance'- both these will give us the 'lay out' of the letter. Fully thought out matter, step-wise written in paragraphs required will give us fine arrangement in a letter. Neatly written with proportionate space for reason based paragraph, will add to the look of the letter.

What does lay-out connote, will be clear from the tabular hints noted below:

Sl. No.	MATTER	POINTS TO BE NOTED
1.	Logical placement	(a) Fine look (b) Begin letter writing after leaving 2 spaces below salutation (c) End each letter above complimentary close leaving 2 spaces (d) Inside address
2.	Sides-spacing	(a) Left and right hand margins should be sufficient (b) 1 inch desirable (c) 1.5 inch wide margin quite common (d) Margin leaving should be proportionate to the top and the bottom space left. For example: 2/3 margin preferred compared to the top and the bottom spacing
3.	Paragraph-spacing preferred	(a) Between paragraphs-single line spacing (b) Letters with less information double line spacing be followed
4.	Indenting	(a) Block or straight edged (b) Indented or stepped in form (c) Semi-blocked or combination form (d) Hanging indention form

ILLUSTRATIVE INDENTIONS

There are different ways in which business letters are written. The contents presentation certainly requires proper arrangement of letter parts and spacing with sufficient margin. Other wise, letter will not attract the attention of the reader and it may look quite clumsy. The types given below will surely suggest different methods of spacing and idea based paragraphs and finally how various parts of the letter should appear. Of course, if we observe the latest preference and trend, complete block form is being much followed by the letter-writing mass in business circle.

Full Block Styles

A ____________________

B ____________________

C ____________________

____

____

D ______________________________

E ______________________________

F ______________________________

____

____

____

G ______________________________

H ______________________________

Indented or Stepped in Form

A ______________________________

____

B ______________________________

C ______________________________

____

____

D ______________________________

E ______________________________

F ______________________________

____

____

____

____

____

____

G ______________________________

H ______________________________

Indented or Stepped in Form

A ______________________________

____

B ____________________

C ____________________

____

____

D ____________________

E ____________________

____

____

____

____

G ____________________

H ____________________

Note: (a) Heading (b) Date (c) Inside address (d) Salutation (e) Subject line (f) Body of the letter (g) Complimentary (h) Signature.

FULL BLOCK FORM

A ____________________

____

B ____________________

C ____________________

____

____

D ____________________

E ____________________

F ____________________

____

____

____

G ____________________

H ____________________

BUSINESS- LETTER PARTS- THEIR DENOTATION IN A SKETCH

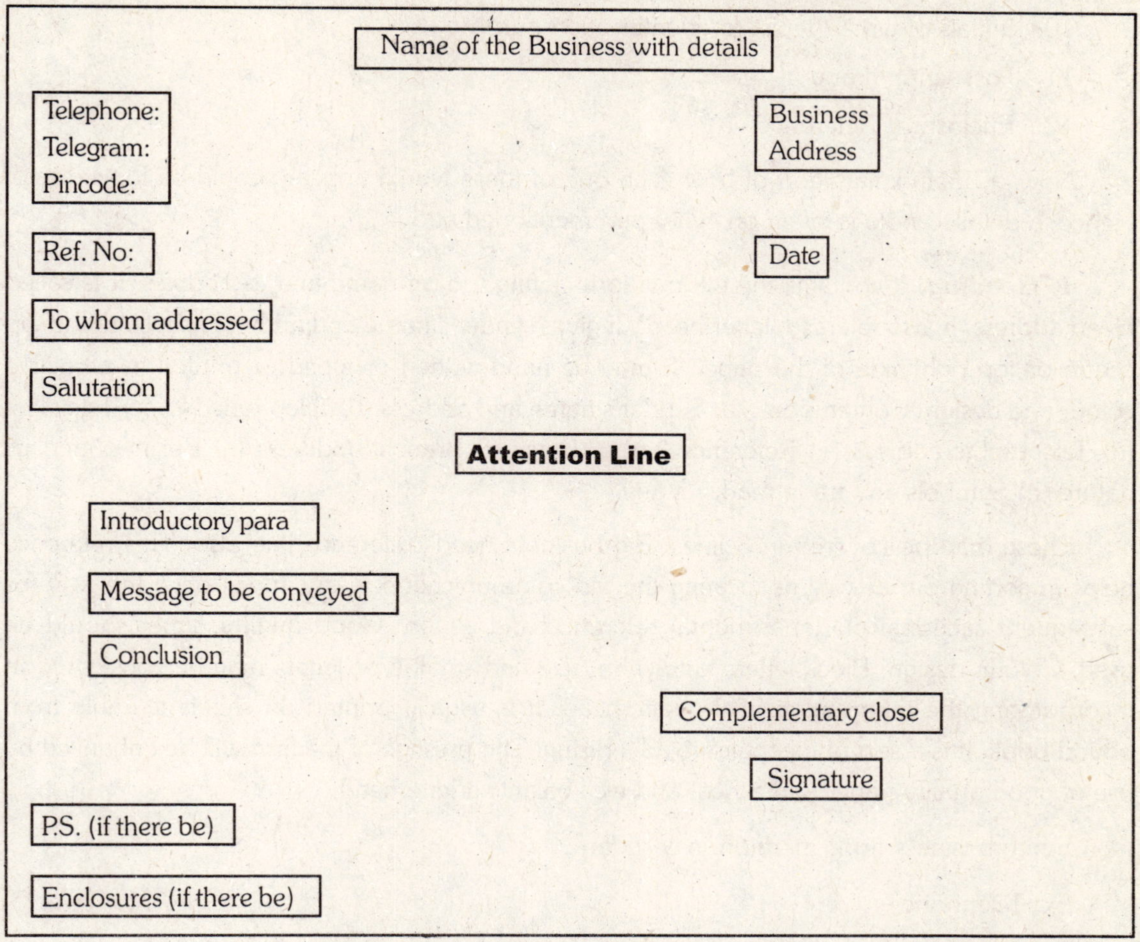

Business letter its split up for a thorough consideration of each part may be named and numbered as follows:

1. Heading (The Head address) (Name of the firm and address) (Letter Head)
2. Date line (The date)
3. Inside Address
4. Attention line
5. Salutation (greeting)
6. Reference (subject line) (Ref. No.) (Capital line)
7. Body of the letter (Essence/Message/ Substance of the letter) (Main part) consisting of introduction, subject matter and conclusion
8. Complimentary close (subscription) (leave taking paragraph)

9. Signature (and the seal)
10. Initials of writer/ typist for identification purpose
11. Post script, if any
12. Enclosure, Reference.

Now, a brief explanation of how each one of these would appear should be looked into. Hence, a detailed note is given on every part mentioned above.

1. Heading: It contains the information relating to firm-name and its address. It is called Head address. It also refers to 'letter-head'. It gives sender's name and address usually at the top centre or top right side of the paper. It may be hand-written or typed or printed in attractive colour and design. Contents are: (a) Sender's name and address (b) Telephone No. (c) Telex No. (d) Telegraphic address (e) Reference No. or Index (f) Branches/address (g) Business and its nature (h) Symbols and trade marks, if any.

These may be covered in 3 lines. Big business needs reference line also. This reference helps in sorting out as well as locating the old communication if any. It will pave the way for subsequent sectional or departmental reference and action. Good quality paper should be used. Colour, design, Block letters, attraction, size and small type letters may be considered in incorporating the information in the letterhead. It is usually printed on sheets tearable from bound book. It is a sort of inexpensive advertising. The prestige of the firm will be enhanced by use of good quality paper and a neat and well balanced letterhead.

Some business firms mention in a square.

Ex: Telephone GRAM :

MURTHY BOOK DEPOT

36, Market Road,

TUMKUR

In you reply please quote F-13/D 1018

here, 'F means file, '13' his file No. and 'D' means despatch and '1018' refers to the despatch No.

Examples:

(a) "PVN/R. K/226" here indications are: Letterwriter= P.V. Narayan R.K.= R. Krishnaswamy, the typist 226= file No.

(b) "FIN/94/91-92"- It means FIN- Finance Department 94= letter bearing no. '91-92' is the concerned year.

2. Date Line: The day, the month and the year of the letter will be mentioned here. It is a detail of identification of letter written on what Date. The day on which information was sent may be easily found out for a *reference* of legal purpose. Right top nook is the proper place for writing the date using five spaces. It captures the reader's attention easily. Spacing between the two numbers should be carefully done. Confusion should be totally avoided by writing the name of the month between the number of the day in the month and the year in which that letter would be written to the *concerned*. It is written five spaces below the heading. Carelessness and hurried nature should be avoided. The exact writing of the date is very important. Date is an essential part of a business. It must be written 3 or 4 spaces below the name of the place. Both the place and the date have an important bearing on the correspondence. These may be a dotted line for date. It acts as a remainder to the typists to type it out. The advantages of date-writing are: (a) Future quick Ref. (b) Prompt action, (c) Systematic and chronological filing of letters. Abbreviations for months should be used. Year should not be cut short. Abbreviations for names of cities are a source of confusion; hence, it should be totally avoided. For example: 'Bg' for Bangalore 'M-lore' Mangalore. Alah: Allahabad, Bomb: Mumbai etc.

Illustrative examples of date-writing in business letters and other types of communication may be well understood from the table given below logically arranged and analysed:

SL.NO.	DATE	WHICH TYPE?	REASONS FOR ACCEPTANCE OR AVOIDANCE
1.	14.6.1998	General	This is to be dropped in correspondence with American companies, because month is stated first in American style. It creates difficulty in typing
2.	14.6.1998	General	Avoid
3.	14.6.1998	General	Avoid
4.	14 Aug.1998	Oxford University American	Not preferred
5.	14 Aug.1998	British (English)	Not preferred as it creates errors and confusion
6.	14 Aug.1998		Preferred because there is no confusion There is clear cut line of thought in the it reader's mind regarding Day, Month and Year. It is popular in U.K.
7.	14 Aug.1998	English	May be used
8	14 Aug.1998	English	May be written
9.	14 Aug.1998	English	May be adapted
10.	14th Aug.1998	General	Avoid in typing

Of all methods in general, American and British styles of writing the date, the best style *or* type or method is the 6th example given in the above Table: it is British and the best method. It has a lot of clarity. It avoids confusion between the day and the month in writing and typing the date.

3. Inside - Address : It means subscription. This gives us the details of addressee. It contains name and address of an individual or corporate body to whom the letter is to be sent. It may be given at the left hand bottom or just above salutation in a letter.

Need: (1) to the correct address (2) to suit to window type envelopes (3) to seek clarification (easy tracing) (4) to locate the addressee with ease for lawful remedy carbon copy may be kept in the file for reference. It should be written below the Reference line, leaving some space. Indented (Step) or Block form may be used starting from left side margin. In indented form, two spaces away from the previous line- beginning in writing or typing the address should be followed. A comma follows each line and a full stop after the last line. In Block form each line begins from margin and no punctuation at the end of each line. It is less time taking job with a neat look. The following Table will help us in avoiding the most common errors committed in writing the inside address of individuals considering their personal, corporate, academic Regal professional degrees and dignity. It will uphold the culture in correspondence and decency in addressing and decorum of the situation. The ordinary courtesy titles are Mr. Esq, Shri. Sri, Mrs. Shrimathi, Miss, Mmes and Messrs.

SL NO.	ABBREVIATION	EXPANSION	TO WHOM TO USE
1. (a)	Mr.	Mister	All the three are used for men married or unmarried
(b)	Esq.	Esquire	
(c)	Shri.	Miss	
2.	Miss		Used for Spinster (or unmarried)
3.	Mrs. Shrimathi	Mistress Shreemathi	Used for a married lady or auspicious woman
4.	Messrs	Messieurs	French word meaning Gentlemen. It is plural form of 'Mr.' It should be added *before* the firms having personal names
5.	Mmes	Mesdames	It is plural of 'Mrs.'
6.	For Professional or a Gentleman	Doctor, Advocate, Engineer, Teacher, CA, ICWA, etc. A.C's etc.	Instead of prefix, Esquire or 'Esq' *or* 'Esqr' should be used.

Details of persons as 'Addressees'- and how address them while writing letters will be clear from the examples given in the following table which is just illustrative but not an exhaustive one:

CASE (QUESTIONS)	WHAT TO DO? (ANSWERS)
1. When should you exclude Esquire? (or 'Esq' or 'Esqr')	If the name is prefixed by 'Mr.'/Shri./Dr./Prof./Capt./Major, Esquire is excluded
2. When do you use 'Esq'?	Before writing down the degrees of a person accorded on him by the Academic Bodies i.e., B.A., B.Com., F.R.C.S., M.B.B.S., Ph.D., etc., the word 'Esq' should be used as P.S. Rama Rao, Esq. M.Com., Ph.D.
3. Messrs. Global Flour Mills 47, Madhugiri Road, Tumkur-2. Is use of 'Messrs' correct here?	'Messrs' or 'M/s' is taken from french word 'Messieurs' meaning 'Gentlemen'. It should not be used before name of firms having impersonal names. Here word 'Messrs' should not be used.
4. Given example for correct use of Messrs.	Messrs Rajna Rayan & *Co.*, 331, Santhepet, Madhugiri, Tumkur Dist,
5. Is the following correct? "Messrs Sir James Blue & Co" 16, Cunningham Road, Bangalore	Messrs should be excluded here because, when Firm's name is no doubt personal but it is prefixed by titles like Sir/ Padmashree/ Padma Bhushan/ Rao Bahadur/ Rajasevasakta/ Vidya Praveena/ Dr.Prof.Rev. Colonel- These are called courtesy titles hence, correct address would be 'Sir James & Co.' here
6. May it be true to say M/S Rao and Murthy Ltd. 21, 8th Cross, D.T. Street, Bangalore-3	'M/s' should not be used before the names of any limited company.
7. How do you' address a firm consisting of Ladies (married) Devi & Rani	Here, we should use abbreviation of 'Mesdames'- Mmes. Devi & Rani
8. If members of firm are spinsters- how do you prefix their membership	Here the word 'Mises' should be prefixed as Misses. Vedavathi and Vidyavanthi
9. When is it befitting to use 'Dr.' as prefix?	If a person is possessing an M.B.B.S., M.D., Ph.D., D. Litt., which are medical or academic degrees of their excellence and veneration, the prefix 'Dr' can be used as Dr. Vanaspathi, Dr Veedhisarathi, etc.
10. Can you use both 'Mr.' and 'Esq' while writing down the address.	Both 'Mr.' and Esq are not used together. The word 'Esq' is used between 'name' and academic degrees. For example: V.N. Padapathi, Esq., or V.N. Padapathi, Esq., Bar-at-Law

11. When should you not use 'Messrs'	It should not be used before (a) an individual (b) unknown officer of firm (c) Impersonal Title (d) when it begins with 'The' or (e) when the courtesy title is included, 'Messrs' should not be used.

A few examples of writing inside Address:

Addressed to a Private Gentleman:

Mr. S. Panchaksharaiah S.
18, Sampige Road, 18,
Bangalore- 560 003

Panchaksharaiah.Esq.,
Sampige Road
Bangalore- 560003

Addressed to married/ unmarried woman:

Miss. Kathyayani,
16, Temple Street,
Koratagere.
Tumkur Dt.

Mrs. Kamala Shankar
Central College,
Bangalore-1

Indians may use following Prefixes
Mr= Shri (Shriman)
Miss= Kum(Kumari)
Mrs= Smt (Shrimathi)

Addressed to a Tradesman

Mr. Jnanaadhipa,
Grantha Trader,
48, Saraswathi Patha,
Vedapura.

Addressed to Professional Men: (Use of Esquire)

B.M. Vidyadhipa, Esq., F.R.C.S.,
Lalbagh Road, Bangalore.

or

S.M. Nyayadhipa, Esq., Bar-at-Law
76, Raja Beedi,
Nyayapura.

Use of Messrs:

(a) Messrs. Raja and Bhoja,
Jupiter Building,
188, Nehru Road, Tiptur.

Messrs not to be used:

(b) The Moola Grantha Company,
Jnaneswara Street,
Sugandhapuri.

(c) Rao Bahadur Amarnath and Sons,
Oldgate,
Rawalpindi.

(d) Sir Issac Pitman & Sons,
Kingsway,
London, W.C.2.

(e) The Gateway of India,
167, Church Street,
Cox Town,
Bangalore.

(f) The Universal Traders,
112, Nariman Road,
Mumbai-17.

(g) The Advertising Manager, The Secretary,
International Instrument Ltd., Lipton Tea Ltd.,
Bangalore. New Delhi-4.

4. Attention Line: If the letter written by us should receive the attention of an individual officer holding a responsible position, then, this is used. It is a specific direction to place the letter to be read by him only. We may write "For the attention of.....or Attention of....." It is written between Inside Address and Salutation. It is underlined. Even on the Envelope it is written. The objects are (a) drawing the attention of a specific officer and (b) quickening the process of settlement, reply, sanction, decision on the matter etc.

Ex. (1) Binny Mills Ltd.
Goodshed Road,
Near Briyond Square,
Bangalore.

For the attention of Mr. P.T. Rangan
Dear Sir,

Ex. (2) Attention: Mr. R.K. Gupta,
Managing Director.

Ex. (3) "For the attention of Dr. Reddy"
M/s. P. Pandit and Co.,
1, Vedavyasa Road,
K.R. Extension,
Tumkur-4.

5. Salutation (Greeting): It is inaugurating our communications with addressee with honour of normal character. It also means greeting. It also implies politeness or affection, custom in business demand us to use permissible word to respect the other party whether an individual or an institution, firm or corporation. On deep analysis, it does not imply personal regard of writer but, it avoids sudden beginning. It validates customary respect to the addressee. It is written after the inside address with double line space. Use of Comma after salutation is commonly followed. American method of putting a colon after greeting is not widely practised. In conversation 'Hello' is used while in written letters, saluations are of varied nature (1) Singular and plural numbers, (2) Degree of respect intended (3) Custom in business (4) Nearness (5) Strangeness (6) Affection to be shown (7) Politeness and (8) Formality. Some of the factors which help us in important points to be noted are (i) When 'dear' is written after 'My', 'd' is not in capital, and (ii) Do not use the singular form of 'Gentleman'.

SL. NO.	NATURE OF ADDRESSES TO USE	WHICH SALUTATION
1.	State Govt. Secretary	Sir
2.	Central Govt. Finance Officer	Sir
3.	Editor of 'Hindustan Times'	Sir
4.	Foreign Ambassador/ Customs Officer	Sir
5.	Businessman/ Trader (ordinary)	Dear Sir ,
6.	Close-contact between writer and receiver	My dear Sir,
7.	A business lady	Madam (rarely used)
8.	Spinster and Married Woman	Dear Madam
9.	A business firm consisting of Ladies	Mesdames (or Ladies)
10.	Companies, Cooperative, Corporations, Associations, Clubs, Committees, Boards, Commissions, Meeting	Dear Sirs (used commonly + collectively) Gentleman (widely used in U.S.A.)
11.	Company Letters	Dear Sirs (Name proceeded by Messrs)
12.	Men in a firm	Dear Sirs/Gentlemen
13.	Writer knows the addressee very well and wants to be amicable and intimate (individually) in Business letters	Dear Mr. Narasimhan, Dear Shri. Srikanth, Dear Mrs. Soubhagya, Dear Smt. Netravathi, Dear Kum. Kantha

14.	For drafting circular and sales letters	My dear Mr. Shambhulinga, Dear Client, Dear Subscriber, Dear Reader,
15.	Women's firm	Mesdames/ Mmes Dear
16.	An official of Chamber of Commerce	Sir
17.	A judge of a High Court Income Tax	Sir
18.	Commissioner	Sir
19.	M.L.A./ M.P.	Dear Sir
20.	Governor of a State in India	May it please your Excellency

6. Reference (Subject Line/Ref. No./ Caption Line): It indicates the theme. It refers to be subject of the letter. It makes the main matter concise and clear. It arrests the attention of businessman in matters of urgency. It is written after salutation. Inward correspondence will be facilitated. It helps filing based on subject. In fact subject and reference go hand in hand. Reference indicates previous reference or letter. Filing will become easy and reply to the letter will also be made easy. Subject heading or Reference briefly said, pinpoints (a) purpose (b) past correspondence (c) easy sorting out in inward section and (d) file-tracing. "One letter, one subject" is the best; it will not pool and perplex the reader. Filing will be complex owing to many matters of divergence being considered in a single letter. Only when the matter is complex in nature, a brief note is essential. When the whole matter is made crystal clear in the first paragraph, there is no need to give subject or reference line in the correspondence. Anyhow, most of it is a matter of custom in trade.

It gives in nutshell what is contained in the main communication of the letter. Reference or Caption line is heavily underlined. It is made distinct placing the words. Re: or Ref: or Sub: before it.

Examples of Reference Making

(a) Dear Sir,

Sub: Issue of circular letter in favour of..............

Ref: Your letter No. RCL/J/21-97 dated 23rd June, 1997

(b) Dear Sir,

Re: Cheque Dishonoured

Ref: Our letter No. NODCD/207/96-97 of 18th May 1997

(c) Dear Sir,

Sub: Clarification of debit of Rs.......

(d) Dear Sir,

Ref: Your Requisition dated 18th May, ...

Thus, the subject line serves the purpose of letting the reader know what the message is about. It saves time.

Examples of where to write/type subject or Reference

(a) The Nirma Trading company 16-A, Gayathrinagar, Old Market, Bangalore.
Attention: The Finance Manager
Dear Sir,
Subject: Remittance by cheque of Rs. 1,40,000 No. V91 CD420067
dt. 16.08.97

(b) Shanno Jewel Works
112, gowrava Rasthe, Maryade Nagar Cross, Ghanagambheera
Extention, Adarshapura.
Attention: Sri. B.S. Maharaj
Subject: Payment of Bill No. p 952 of 24th October, 1996.
Dear Sirs/ Madam,

(c) Commonest Way
Dear Sir,
Subject: Proposed campaign Expenditure.
Reference: The Advertisement in "The Economic Times" of 18th June, 97.

7. Body of the letter (Essence/Message/Substance/Main text): It contains information proper for communication with addressee. It is the most important part. It begins usually after the saluation ends. Left side margin is allowed. It contains the main message to be conveyed to the respondent. It may be a fresh item of information or in response to his previous letter. Hence, it needs careful organisation and arrangement. It is chiefly divided into 3 stages:

(a) Opening/ introductory/ previous reference/ gists of past letter- why continuity etc.

(b) The Main part/ important message and

(c) Closing paragraph/conclusion/ expectations/ wishes/ intentions etc.

Opening paragraph to introduce writer's intention. Reader's attention will be drawn. It expresses happiness, thankfulness and receipt to previous letter. Reader's interest will be arrested at once. It produces zeal. It makes the reader go inquisitive. It suffices anticipation. If letter should be a solid mass of data it will be difficult to digest. It should be interesting, inquisitive, plain and perfect. For a short letter, one paragraph constitutes the body of the letter. If several matters are mentioned, each matter should be dealt with in a separate paragraph. Paragraphs should be arranged in logical order with a view to presenting the facts in the best possible way. Each paragraph should be attractive in appearance and informative in content.

(a) It should begin after salutation. One inch from the left margin should be provided. Just below salutation, it starts. Arrange the paragraphs neatly.

(b) Adopt conversational style.

(c) Let the beginning be amicable and polite.

(d) Be brief and plain to arrest the mind of the receiver of message.

(e) Don't use meaningless and heckneyed phrases which are non-current, circumlocutory and ineffective.

(f) Avoid verbose and Victorian era phrases which are vain.

(g) You should not begin your letter with a sense of regret or rejection.

A few examples for rubber stamp opening paragraphs are:

1. In reply to your kind favour, we beg to reply.........
2. Acknowledging your letter of......
3. Yours to hand........
4. We are in receipt of.........
5. We have noted the contents of your letter......

A few examples for better expression are:

1. Thank you very much for your order dated.....
2. Thank you for your letter dated.....
3. We have received your letter dated..... on.....
4. We received your letter dated..... only yesterday.....
5. We read your letter dated..... and, fully we have enlisted your needs.

Main Paragraph: It contains the main message. Unrelated matters should be left out. Each para should deal with only one aspect of one subject on hand. For different subjects, different letter should be written There may be several letters in one envelope. Main paragraph may have several sub-headings. In the body of the letter, the main paragraph resembles the heart of the message. Subject- matter is found in the main paragraph. Main message must be faultless. It should be perfect and complete.

Closing Paragraph: It should express the concluding wish/ direction/ anticipation/ action of writer to addressee who will read the letter. It is a summary paragraph. It gives a final finishing touch to the letter. Writer's action should be written in understandable and firm language. Stereotyped phrases should be avoided.

Examples of Stereotyped phrases are:

1. Assuring of you of our best attention at all times.
2. Awaiting the favour of your esteemed commands.
3. Thanking you in anticipation of a favourable reply.
4. Soliciting a continuance of past favours etc.
5. Hoping to hear from you at an early date.

Concluding paragraph should be forceful and convincing and simple. Courtesy, expression of hope for favourable reply, assuring addressee of attention may not be fully out of place but, it should be thoughtful and not a repetition of state and worn out phrases.

8. Complimentary close (Subscription): It is 'leave taking'. It is a method of ending the letter with politeness, two spaces below the last line of the body of the letter. There should be agreement in tone between salutation and complimentary close. It is a form of saying 'good-bye'. It is written on the right hand side down the last line of the body of the letter. The commonest complimentary close is "Yours faithfully" 'y' should be in capital letter and there should be no apostrophe in the word 'yours' before the consonant 's'. It is also called 'subscription' or formal leave taking. A comma should be used at the end. This close should not be detached from the body of the letter in case 'carry over' or shifting the message over a different page.

Common examples of complimentary close are: Yours faithfully, Yours sincerely. Yours truly, Yours cordially. It is a courteous phrase written in a distinct line, above the signature at the bottom of the letter. The complimentary close is a polite way of ending a letter.

Complimentary close must be in agreement with the salutation used in the letter.

Sl. No.	LETTERS WRITTEN (NATURE)	SALUTATION	COMPLIMENTARY CLOSE
1.	BUSINESS LETTERS (Seller to buyer)	Dear Sir/Dear Sirs/ Dear Madam/ Gentlemen	Yours Sincerely
2.	SUPERIOR (Subordinate to Officer)	Sir/Madam/ Sirs/Mesdames	Yours Respectfully, or Yours faithfully,
3.	PRIVATE AND BUSINESS LETTERS (Between X and Y)	Dear Mr	Yours Sincerely,
4.	STRANGE BUSINESSMEN (Without mutual knowledge) (X and Y)	Dear Sir/ Dear Madam	Yours truly,
5.	BETWEEN FRIENDS (X and Y)	Dear Sir/ My Dear Babu	Yours Sincerely,

6.	BETWEEN VERY CLOSE FRIENDS AND RELATIVES (PRIVATE)	Dear Venugopal My dear Narayan	Yours affectionately,
7.	From Business Club (to associate)	Dear Member	Yours Sincerely,
8.	For Sales (to customers)	Dear Customer	Yours Sincerely,
9.	Newspaper (to Readers from Businessman)	Dear Customer	Yours Sincerely,
10.	Magazine (From seller to customer)	Dear Reader	Yours Sincerely,
11.	From Subordinate (to superior in Business Management)	Sir	Yours faithfully
12.	To High dignitary from an individual	Sir	Yours faithfully,
13.	From student publisher to college Principal	Sir/Respected Sir/ Prof.	Yours Respectfully,
14.	For Air conditioning sales	-	yours Colly,
15.	For food items sales	-	yours Tastily,

Note: I am. I remain, etc. followed by 'Sir' (or gentlemen) are some times used in official correspondence with sir (or gentlemen) as a salutation. E.g.

Sir,

I am,

Your obedient servant

Now, this salutation is not in use nor it is desirable.

Signature (and the seal): It means a signed name. The writer by writing his name himself gives the assent to the subject-matter of the letter. It is the last part of the letter and is placed after the complimentary close. Illegible signature demands the writer to write in Block letters his full name. Firm's or company's seal may be rubber-stamped, if he writes and signs for it. The name should appear below the name of that firm or company. The facsimile (of the signature) may be used on behalf of the letter- writer on approval only.

Signature and its legal effects: Signature is any indication/ symbol/ letter/ mark by which the writer assumes responsibility for all that the letter contains. Name or mark designated by writer may be written or made in any manner. Law permits a binding to be created on all the persons concerned with business deal of a firm. Usually, about six spaces are left for the hand-written signature. There is no legal direction as to how to affix the signature. The manner of symbolising/ -marking/ affixing or denoting depends entirely on the individual. If the letter is written by some one other than the true writer, when the true dealer is illiterate and cannot write the letter, then, an illiterate's lefthand thumb impression is to be obtained in place of his signature and the same should be attested by the practical writer of the letter who should have authority as per the letters of law of the land or circumstances.

HOW TO SIGN

BUSINESS CONCERN	HOW SIGNATURE MADE
I. *A Sole Trader:*	
(a) Trading under his own name	Yours faithfully, K. Krishna
(b) Trading under the assumed name of Tulasi and Co.	Yours faithfully, For Tulasi and Co., K. Krishna
(c) If owner is a lady not married	(Miss) R.P. Sathyabhama Proprietor
(d) If owner is a lady married	(Mrs) Rukmini Krishna Proprietor
II. *A Firm:*	
(a) Soma and Bheema & Co., (B.Soma and S. Bheema are partners)	Yours faithfully, For Soma and Bheema & Co., S.Bheema or Yours faithfully, For Soma and Bheema & Co., B. Soma
(b) Per. Pro. or P.P. (Latin origin) (per procurationem = As an Agent for)	Yours faithfully, Per pro. Vakkannalambodaya & Co. Shambavi
Firm	
Vakkannalamboaya & Co. Shambavi- an employee (Legally authorized partnership signature)	Yours faithfully, P.P. Shambavi,Vakkannalayboaya & Co.
(c) A clerk or subordinate signs routine/ numerous/unimportant letters and imprints it with Rubber stamp and initials it proceeded by 'per' / 'for'	Lokavichitra and Co. per K. Pinakadhara or Lokavichitra and Co. for K. Pinakadhara

III. A Limited Company	
(a) Manager/ M.D./ Secretary/Direct or has a power of Attorney or from a custom.per pro. indicates legal authority)	For Urvashi & Co. Ltd. G. Sundareshwara Secretary Per pro. Soundarya & Co. Ltd. L. Sarvajna Per pro. Vaikhari Bhashya and Co. S.R.N.Murthy Managing Director The Building Materials, Ltd. B. Kulkarni Secretary B.K. Ranjan Secretary
(b) Signature indicating the responsibility of the company	Yours faithfully, For Lotus & Co., Ltd., P. Neelamegha Sales Manager
(c) Signature indicating Individual responsibility	Yours faithfully, S. Gajamukha Advertising Manager Sugandhadravya & Co. Ltd. Yours faithfully, for Johnson and Stephenson Ltd. B. Brown (Manager) Yours faithfully, M.K. Kariyappa (P.A. to prinicipal)

Signature must be in ink. It is the distinguishing mark. Owner, or his Agent or officer duly authorised can sign the letters, cards, representations, applications, Bills, Invoice, cheques, memos, circulars, reports, accounts, Ledgers, statements, Notes, Bonds, certificates, deeds, rules and regulations copies, returns, etc. making it clear in what status, he is signing the document. As proprietor, one has enormous powers in law; but, as an Agent, one should go by what law says, 'for and on behalf of or 'per pro' should be administered with care and caution within the ambit of authority extended to him orally, documentarily, customarily, circumstantially, unavoidably, of course, always lawfully for Business. There should be no malafide intention on per. pro signature.

10. *Reference Initials*: Quite often, Letter dictator's and typist's initials are placed in the bottom left hand corner in capital letters. It may be put under the date also. Some special squares may be printed for this purpose. With a view to fixing up the responsibility, initials are inserted in the Box, meant for the purpose. In the left hand margin one or to spaces below the signature, these marks are put. It is now a common practice.

For example:

M.R. Saraswathi (dictator)

G. Rao (typist)

then, identification marks may be noted in any one of the following ways:

1. MRS GR
2. MRS : GR
3. GS

11. *Post script (if any)*: Its abbreviation is "P.S". Its latin origin is "Postscriptum" which means "Written afterwards". Extra matter to be communicated will be found written below the signature. P.S. indicates that writer is careless. It creates bad impression. It means after thoughts. It means that letter writer had no planning. It indicates hurry and carelessness in composition. The difference in the subject-matter or the receipt of information after finishing the letter, under 'exceptional clause' may have to-be written as the post script. Only the original letter writer can write 'P.S'. He should sign or initial it to avoid mischief. Post scripts should be numbered. It is better to avoid. The whole letter may be rewritten avoiding P.S.

Post script is a bit or writing added to the letter after the signature. It has no complimentary close. It is a small bit of information. It is not a part of the main message but an extra point which was forgotten. When the writer likes to give information to draw the reader's attention effectively P.S. is used. P.S. leaves an indelible impression. P.S. may be a friendly note. It may be in 1-3 lines. P.S. may be used for conveying urgent information. The new trend however advocates the use of P.S. as being more effective than the letter itself.

Example:

(a) Godrej share price shot upto Rs. 390.

(b) Purchase held up. Draft wanted for Rs. 10,000/- soon.

(c) Don't forget, sales close on the 14th.

12. *Superscription:* It means "that which is written outside or above something". It indicates To address' written on envelope. It helps the letter to be delivered to the correct addressee without difficulty of searching and tracing. Address must be accurate and complete. Use of window envelope with a transparent panel avoids the writing of address of addressee for the second time on the envelope.

13. ***Enclosure (s) ("Encl"/"Encls")*** : It means paper, record, document, cheque, Bill, statement, voucher, receipt, catalogue, price list, check list, railway receipt, shipping note, lorry receipt, share warrant, share certificate, air ticket, deed, bond, cash memo, prospectus, etc., which are enclosed or attached or pinned to the covering letter or main letter and are sent to the addressee. It warns and guides inward clerk to check up the enclosures as might be recorded and enlisted in the letter at left hand bottom.

ESSENTIALS OF A GOOD BUSINESS LETTER

The letter-writing as a method of written communication is still important. The progress in science and technology is well seen in telecommunication methods. The words uttered in talk may go out of memory sooner or later; but, anything expressed in writing will continue to be a binding force. That is why the letter is still a significant method for message to be conveyed. With the rapid changes in scientific and socio-economic fields, the styles in communication and types of messages have become different. Business letter is scribe's ambassador or corporate messenger in words. A letter may make or mar the writer's future stay in business. It may build up a good image in the minds of readers and public in general. Reading all the past correspondence may give us the real events and their course. This background gives a dependable picture to the writer to write only the relevant in his letter. Letter writing has following advantages:

1. It helps personal contact
2. It serves as a record maintenance
3. It is a means of keeping the parties informed as and when change in business takes place
4. For attending to enquiries and quotations
5. Potential customers may be contacted
6. Dealing with complaints will go easy
7. Making status enquiries will become a dependable one
8. Creation and maintenance of good will is possible
9. Writer can project a favourable image in the minds of the readers.

Business correspondence has a specific part in a deal. It must achieve the purpose. It may create responsibilities in the eyes of law: Therefore, Business letter-writing demands of the writer a series of essentials or characteristic features enlisted below. Each one of these should be considered in detail to grasp the essentials fully well.

I. According to James Stephenson, (in his Book "Principles and Practice of Commercial Correspondence" (Chapter III, p-17-III Edition)) the essentials or characteristics of a good style are:

   (a) Pertinency (b) Clearness (c) Brevity (d) Courtesy (e) Orthography and punctuation

II. According to M. Aldertopink and S.E. Thomas, (in their Book "English Grammar, Composition and Correspondence") the essentials of a good letter are:

(a) Knowing what to say (b) Clearness (c) Conciseness or Brevity (d) Accuracy of statement (e) Courtesy phrasing (f) Attractive wording and appearance (g) Commercial English (its connotation and relevance) (h) Forcefulness (i) Spelling, punctuation and writing.

The Four Cs of the Business Letter indicate four essentials of a business letter. These features make the business letters effective and purposeful.

They are:
(1) Correctness
(2) Clarity
(3) Conciseness and
(4) Courtesy

The Eight Cs of Commercial Correspondence : These are essential features of good business letters to be borne in mind.

They are :
(1) Correctness (2) Clearness
(3) Conciseness (4) Courtesy
(5) Completeness (6) Concreteness
(7) Comprehensiveness and (8) Consideration.

Before offering a brief explanation of all the essentials noted so far, some rearrangement is required. Hence, the following list. This list, gives almost all the features of effective business letters.

1. Promptness
2. Knowing what to say (Subject-matter or message to be conveyed by letter)
3. Pertinency (Relevance/ Relation/ Concern/ Suitability)
4. Appropriate tone and language (contextual expression)
5. Correctness (in appearance, language and information)
6. Clarity (clarity/ completeness and accuracy in thought and expression)
   (a) Grammatical acceptability
   (b) Dubious use of pronouns
   (c) Dichotomy in connotation (words with duality in meaning)
   (d) Perplexity in thinking
7. Conciseness (Brevity): Avoid
   (a) Repetitive use of words (Tautology)
   (b) Redundancy use of words (Pleonasm)
   (c) Circumlocution (Verbosity)

8. Courtesy (hearty kindness and consideration and use of touchy phrases)
9. Adroitness (Tact+ Strategic shrewdness)
10. Polite, pleasant and positive approach
11. Good bye' to Jargon (or Victorian style/commercial English)
12. Forceful expression (emphatic and persuasive)
13. Coherence (connection/ logical flow/ corollary)
14. Character (mark of individuality/ originality/ arresting reader's attention)
15. Amicable and optimistic approach.

1. *Promptness:* It refers to punctuality in providing immediate response to letters. Back reference will take much time. In case reply is delayed, at least a word of acknowledgment is essential. It will certainly create a favourable and good impression on the mind of the reader.

2. *Knowing what to say:* Writer should know what he wants to convey. He must grasp all the facts and collect all the figures. Ideas should be logically arranged. Confused expression is the result of confusion of ideas. Details to be dealt with must be fully assimilated. Clear mapping out of the full subject in the mind's eye is an absolute need for correspondence. Firm's policies and the customer's needs will help us in writing a letter with confidence. Briefly, it means subject matter and main message to be conveyed by the letter must be clear.

3. *Pertinency*: It should be relevant in content and suitable for the purpose. It is the result of thorough knowledge of the subject matter. Irrelevant and intricate phraseology should be dispensed with. Expressions of sensitiveness, irritability and satirical remarks, or gibes should not be used. It should be relevant and within the framework of exact message.

4. *Appropriate Tone and Language*: It means circumstantial expression. Fine feelings will lay the track for good customers. Tone of the letter differs from occasion like affectionate, lovely, jovial, amicable, illustrative, mercantile, primary, gracious, scholarly, officious, telegraphic, legalistic, regal, medical, pragmatic, sataric, indicative, indignant, repungant, poetic, philanthropic, exhaustive, admonitory, pious, piognant, pitiable, dependable, suspicious, believable, beneficial and so forth. High sounding words may detract the reader. So be simple, normal and humane in use of words.

5. *Correctness*: Message will be spoilt by incorrect language and mutilated look of the letter. Damage will be done to the image of the writer. Wrong meaning may be conveyed. Typing and grammatical errors will create a bad impression. Improper margin and careless spacing of paragraphs will make the letter look shabby. Incorrect information will devour time, fame and profit. 'Wrong' in a letter will destroy confidence. Mis-spelling and punctuation errors will not only mar the message but also, bulldoze the business. The mode of expression should not be rude for a businessman, what he says is very important. Direct, precise and forceful style is to be adopted. Language of conversation, free from pompous style is appropriate to business letters. Successful writer should avoid commercial English. Cause of errors may be: (a) Carelessness (b) Arrogance and (c) Presumption. Errors may victimise letter writer through costly law-suits. Great care is to be taken in writing date, quantity, measurement and prices. A keen observation, checking and re-ticking off will pave the way for correctness.

6. *Clearness*: It means clarity. Words and sentences must be arranged to convey the exact meaning. Choice of words and phrases must be set in meaningfully. Ambiguous words must be omitted. Precise expression avoids Business letter does not demand redundant words or flowery expressions because, it leads to mis-interpretation. Sentences should be clear-cut. At one persual, the reader must catch the essence of the letter. Clearness indicates absence of ambiguity; ambiguity is due to word-commission, punctuation-fault, and arrangement-fault in words "Gentlemen should have good manners while the businessman should have correctness". Any letter which does not demand repeated reading is said to have clearness in message. Clearness also means completeness and accuracy in thought and expression. Unintelligible letter proves detrimental to the writer. Measures to achieve clearness are:

(a) Words should not displease the ear.

(b) Pronouns should be clearly used.

(c) Ambiguous words should not be used.

(d) There should not be incoherent thinking and unplanned writing. Clear writing presupposes clear thinking.

(e) Retentive memory and logical order in the form of synopsis will lend to clarity in matter.

(f) Inclusion of essentials and omission of irrelevant matter should be confirmed and

(g) Topic-wise space and para- arrangement will avoid post-scripts.

7. *Conciseness*: Businessmen have no time to devote it to reading and mastering the contents. Therefore, brevity is absolutely essential. A business letter must stick to the point. Laws of grammar and customs of courtesy should be consistent. It should not be at the expense of grammatical accuracy and good style. Redundancy of expression is objectionable specially in business letters. Time is valuable for both the writer and the reader.

Measures to achieve the concise may be stated as follows:

(a) Avoid tautology or repetition of words which will not enrich the meaning.

(b) Avoid pleonasm (needless adding of words)

(c) Avoid verbosity (Round about/ circumlocutory/unnecessary words)

(d) Avoid vague words (words with no clear meaning)

(e) Brevity in expression effectively wins the attention of the reader.

(f) Don't use telegraphic and stenographic language.

(g) Try to be factual and frank.

Expressions to be avoided are: (Redundancy)

1. We are both agreed
2. Our entire monopoly
3. Closely united together

(Extravagant expressions of pleasure, sorrow etc.)

4. Exceedingly glad
5. Wonderfully good
6. Immensely popular
7. "The police officer was not less desirous of punishing the shouters than his superior" (Not sounding well)
8. "The devil trembles when he sees the sanctimonious person upon his knees" (Ambiguous use of pronoun 'his')
9. "If the Lad left her guardian he would breathe last" (Who would die is to clear, in place of he guardian should be put)
10. Mr. Durbhiksha toiled hard to get a quarter lakh during the recent years which he squandered in Amritsar. (Which refers to 'year' or 'money;. It should be either (a) During the last year which he spent in Amritsar, he earned Rs. 25,000 or (b) During the year he earned Rs. 25,000 which he spent in Amritsar.)
11. Let him go not kill him (where to put comma?) It may be (a) Let him go, not kill him or (b) Let him go not, kill him
12. Go slow work in progress (Where to put comma/ fullstop) go, slow in progress (non-sense)

Hence, it should be, "go-slow. Work in progress".

13. Avoid Use

(a) In a considerable no. of cases	(a) Often
(b) In close proximity to	(b) Nearly
(c) Enclosed, please find herewith	(c) Enclosed
(d) Express a preference for	(d) Prefer
(e) Give consideration	(e) Consider
(f) Arrive at a decision	(f) decide
(g) Cut off deliberation and come to	(g) decision-making the conclusion
(h) Safe and secure	(h) Safe or secure

(i) To speak all at one together (Tautology)	(i) To sum up
(j) More preferable (pleonasm)	(j) More desirable or preferable
(k) A sole monopoly (pleonasm)	(k) Monopoly
(l) A false lie (pleonasm)	(l) a lie
(m) I think it proper and advisable to intimate you the fact that while I was engaged in examining my books of account etc.	(m) I like to inform inform you that our account shows that.....

8. *Courtesy*: Whatever the occasion, a business letter must be courteous. Courtesy is behavioural consideration and sympathy. It refers to amicable and kind attitude in a person. Language, style and tone will reveal the personality of business entity. Soft words kill anger in a person. Courtesy defeats grudging. Courtesy does not mean servitude. Courtesy is the lubricant that keeps the wheels of business moving smoothly and without friction. Courtesy distinguishes a gentleman from a boon. Courtesy brings willing and enthusiastic co-operation from the staff. Politeness signifies merely refinement and good manners but, courtesy implies kindness, and hearty consideration. It helps business flourish.

Occasions to show courtesy are:

(a) Settlement of long overdue Account.

(b) Putting forth a claim for damages.

(c) Threatening criminal proceedings.

(d) Shortage or non-delivery of goods.

(e) Shortage or non-delivery of goods.

(f) Accusing the sender of gross negligence.

Courtesy requires a general civility of tone. Courtesy does not mean use of superflous words. Courtesy means human sympathy and good will - a must for business to grow prosperous.

Example of courtesy are : Use of words like please, sorry, thank you, appreciate, grateful etc.

9. Adroitness: It means 'Tact or Tactfulness' or strategy, No businessman should use harsh and unkind words. Such a letter will give rise to displeasure, disagreement and damage to the business. Use always common words. Never pick a row with any customer. Never be quarrelsome. Don't invite or involve in altercations, rebuttal, rebuke, impeachment, serfdom, self-praise, acrimony, sychophancy, excessive grace, exaggeration enthralment, egoism etc. "Be shrewd: Don't be shrewish. Be simple : Don't be a simpleton'. Allow the brain to function in a tranquil way to accomplish the purpose in a tactful way to earn profit.

10. *Polite, Pleasant and Positive Approach:* Sometimes, plain style or no will push the business to nook. Straight negative reply may etc. customer's mind, he may go away from us.

Pleasant words used in a sole monopoly giving a reply will keep at bay the devil of danger. Disagreement complaint handling needs a lot of care. Negation will create irritation. Negative response in a letter demands polite and pleasant communication Dexterity of letter writer alone will convince the reader. Saying 'No' and still retaining "good will" is normally very difficult for any trader. Arrogance and incivility will make him disappear from business sooner or later. So always express your inability to be of service to the customer in a polite and pleasant way. You should not intend hurting his feelings on any account.

11. *'Good Bye' to Jargon*: 'Jargon' means useless and round about use of words. In another sense, 'Jargon' is also meant 'Business English'. It is handed down from early Victorian period. It is a mass of insensible and unconvincing conventions. These, in course of time, have become 'machine-made'. These are called 'stereo-typed phrases'. It is also called 'commercialese'. It shows elaborate politeness and an air of importance. Se ni-legal terms are prolonged in use. It is full of falsity and surrender in style. They express insincere submission. It is feelingless and unnecessary way of writing. It injects a submission. It injects a dramatic sense of status and royal tradition in addressing and informing. These are 'stock phrases.' It must be substituted by frank and clear cut English used in personal interviews. Commercial English is said to be objectionable to all who have the purity of the language at heart. It is contrary to the true interests of commercial life. It encourages the use of dry and meaningless formulae. Therefore, we must now, encourage vigorous language. A businessman should write a vivid and well expressed letter.

12. *Forceful Expression*: It refers to the ability to use appropriate expression and careful arrangement of thoughts in a logical flow. It is necessary for difficult and prolonged negotiation. A strongly worded letter may force the customer to come to an agreement. Steps necessary to attain a degree of force in communication, that too, in writing are:

(a) Clear and concise idea

(b) No deviation from the theme of the letter

(c) Arrangement of facts on a track of logic and law. Of course, the 'forceful expression' is the result of excellence in grammar, composition, vocabulary, oratory and orthography.

13. *Coherence:* It means connection, concern, relation, logical flow, corollary, relevance, consistency, pertinance etc. A good letter needs planning. Ideas of different nature should be well connected in a coherent manner in different paragraphs. It should eliminate confusion. Step wise mention is necessary. Each paragraph should be impregnated with meaning easily understood by an ordinary reader.

14. *Character*: It is an essential feature, nature, quality, or mark an individual writer. The style of writing should arrest the reader's mind. Planning and composition will create a distinguishing mark even in written All people cannot have same modes of expression. The knowledge of science of sentence formation, wide reading, reference to lexicon, need to create novel expression, habitual deep thinking, cultivating the skill of clear communication - all these are to be found in a good correspondence even in the field of elite business deals.

15. Amicable and Optimistic Approach: Be confident, plan to avoid hatred, ill will and uncertainty. A sane behaviour and acceptable look and smile are never mistaken even by illiterate customer. Businessman should have a band of reliable and respectable co-dealers who can provide him with shelter. He should be quite friendly in words and facial expression. He should never blindly welcome failure; rather, he should avoid it by being shrewd throughout. He should not use alien, strange, shameful or satiric words in his written correspondence even by oversight. He must be amicable and optimistic always with a cheer.

STUDY QUESTIONS

Section A

(2 Marks Questions - Answer in 4 lines each)

1. What do you mean by structure of a Business letter?
2. What is physical appearance of letter?
3. Write about the quality of paper you use for a Business letter.
4. What does letterhead connote?
5. What colour does suit a business letter?
6. Does 'typing' outdate hand-written letter? why?
7. Explain the significant role of folding a business letter and mention the process involved.
8. What is the use of 'Window Envelope'?
9. Mention 4 points on layout of a letter in Business
10. Draw lines for Block form, semi Block form, indented (or stepped) form, Hanging indention form, full block form, and indicate headings.
11. Sketch out a business letter denoting its parts.
12. Mention any 4 parts of a Business letter and give the meaning of each in a line.
13. Mention the contents found in a complete Heading of a Business letter.
14 Write out a model Heading of an imaginary company of your choice.
15. Write a brief note on "Heading" of a Business letter.
16. What do you mean by "Date line"?
17. Mention the advantages of date-writing in a Business letter.
18. Give 4 examples of date writing in a Business letter.

19. Are 'Subscription' and Inside Address' analogous? Write a few lines about it.
20. Is 'Inside Address' necessary in a Business letter?
21. What is the need of Inside Address in a Business letter?
22. Give an example for 'inside address' illustrative example and punctuate it as per rules of grammar.
23. Give 4 examples of the ordinary courtesy titles.
24. When do you use 'Esq' and 'Messrs'?
25. What do you mean by 'Mmes' and 'Messierus'?
26. X is a fellow of ICWAI., and ACS., what courtesy title do you use for him ? Write his imaginary inside Address.
27. Write down the degrees MBBS, Ph.D. attached to a name properly and punctuate.
28. When should you exclude 'Esq'?
29. What do you know about 'Messieurs'?
30. Devi and Rani are partners. How do you address them in a Business letter? Give an example there of.
31. 'X' and 'Y' are spinster - partners in a firm. What prefix do you write in a letter of Business addressed to them ?
32. When should you not use Messrs ?
33. Write imaginary addresses of 'a private gentleman' and a Tradesman'
34. What is 'Attention line' in a business letter?
35. Does 'greetings go with salutation'?
36. What salutation do you use for 'Editor' of a news paper and for an Ambassador to a country?
37. What are the factors considered in deciding upon the type of salutation.
38. Indicate the salutations for
    (a) Corporate Body
    (b) Client
    (c) Income Tax commissioner
    (d) An official of chamber of commerce.
39. What does "Reference" mean?
40. What does 'Reference' pinpoint?
41. What is 'subject line'?
42. What is 'caption line'?

43. Give an example of Reference - making for 'circular letter issued' and 'cheque dishonoured'.

44. Give an example for writing 'the Reference along with inside Address to the Nirma Trading Co., and Shanno Jewel works.

45. Give an example for the commonest way of writing 'subject' and Ref'. in a letter.

46. What does body of the business letter contain?

47. What points do you consider to write the message of business letter effectively?

48. Give 2 examples for Rubber stamp opening paragraphs.

49. Give 2 examples for better expression for opening paragraph.

50. Give two examples for stereotyped phrases in the closing paragraph of a business letter.

51. What is complimentary close?

52. What do you mean by subscription?

53. Give 4 common example of complimentary close.

54. State the salutation and complimentary close for any two of the following in a business letter
    (a) Seller to buyer
    (b) Between strange businessmen
    (c) From club to a member
    (d) Book-publisher to a college professor.

55. What do you mean by the 'Signature and the seal' in a business letter?

56. Write about legal effects of signature in a business letter.

57. Give one examples each for any two of the following
    (a) Sole Trader
    (b) Firm
    (c) Agent of a firm
    (d) a limited company.

58. What are identification-marks in a letter?

59. What is 'post scriptum'? Quote an exception circumstance when it may be deemed allowable.

60. Write two examples for post script.

61. What is superscription?

62. What is 'transparent panel' in an Envelop?

63. What do you know of 'Ends'?

64. Mention any eight of 'Ends'?

65. Just mention any 4 essentials of a Business letter.

66. Mention any 4 advantages of letter writing business.

67. Jot down the four Cs of a business letter.

68. Enlist the 'eight Cs' of commercial correspondence.

69. Mention any four occasions when the tone the letter varies.

70. Mention any 4 measures to achieve conciseness in a business letter.

71. Mention any 4 measures to achieve 'clearness' in Business communication.

72. Give two examples for 'Redundancy'.

73. Give two examples for extravagant expression of pleasure or sorrow.

74. Give an example for ambiguous use of pronoun 'his'.

75. Give an example for ambiguous use of 'which'.

76. Use of comma may prove one's life, show it in an example with a change of placement of comma.

77. Use acceptable one word for the following avoidable phrases
    (a) In close proximity to
    (b) Cut off deliberation and come to conclusion
    (c) Express a preference for
    (d) Give consideration to

78. Give two examples of pleonasm in a business letter.

79. Mention 4 occasions to show courtesy in a business letter.

80. Write 4 suitable examples to indicate courtesy in a word or two.

81. What is 'Adroitness' a in business letter?

82. What is 'Jargon' in a business letter?

83. Mention 4 steps to achieve 'forceful expression' in a business letter.

84. What is 'character' in a business letter?

85. What do you mean by optimistic approach in a business letter?

Section B

(8 Marks Questions - Answer in 30 lines each)

1. Give specific Inside address, salutation and complimentary close to (any two)
    (a) The commissioner of Bangalore city
    (b) A popular civilian
    (c) An Agricultural field officer in a Bank
    (d) A share-dealer
    (e) A Medical Representative.

2. Give the appropriate complimentary close and signature of letters written by (any three)
   (a) A customs officer
   (b) State Finance Corporation
   (c) A partner in Flour Mill
   (d) A dealer in steel equipment
   (e) Life Insurance Corporation of India
   (f) State Trading Corporation
   (g) A member of the Stock Exchange.
3. Sketch a well suited letter head for
   (a) An Agro Corporation
   (b) Fertiliser dealer
   (c) Ready made garments shop
   (d) Cement Manufacturer
   (e) A paper mill.
4. Write brief notes on any 4 of the following:
   (a) Heading
   (b) Subscription
   (c) Jargon in Business
   (d) Per pro signatures
   (e) Complimentary close
   (f) Postscripts
   (g) Body of the letter and its importance
   (h) "Courtesy as soul of commercial correspondence
   (i) Write about Reference Number and its use
5. Name the parts of a good business letter and draw a diagram indicating the position of each in the letter.

*****

CHAPTER 3

ACCOUNTS CORRESPONDENCE

- Letters Pertaining to Collection of Dues from Customers
- Bank Correspondence
- Issues of Letters of Credit
- Insurance Correspondence

Letters to customers regarding dues – follow up, Letters to banks regarding overdrafts, cash credit and account current. Letters to insurance and payment, renewal of insurance policy, claims and their settlement, Letters to public authoritieslike P.F. Commissioner, P & T, – regarding payment of P.F. contributions, installation of new connections and payment of telephone bills, payment of sales tax and tax deducted at source.

LETTERS PERTAINING TO COLLECTION OF DUES FROM CUSTOMERS

Credit is the cornerstone of a commercial concern to carry on the trade function in the modern world. 'Cash and Carry' has become an outdated slogan. The present business is patronised by customers who support the philosophy of come, confirm, collect, carry and cash down later on, on being satisfied.

Production in anticipation of customers' desires, perennial flow of goods, high level competition, increase in the complex nature of fashionable articles, warehouse problems, apprehension of delicate goods being spoilt, mutilated, degraded, deteriorated, damaged, rusted and finally rejected always compel the sellers to resort to honouring customers to value their postponed payments insipid of spot physical delivery of goods. It is exactly here the concept of credit, compulsion for credit, and conferring of credit will emerge in the field of business. Of course, credit enhances business without spot cash collection. Credit needs a cautious policy adoption in any business. The natural tendency, conduct, demeanor and dignity of individual will provide us the basis of assessment - whether to grant credit or not, unlike conventional policy of cash payment or no customer at all, has paved the way for a sort of welcome to the world of credit. It is an unavoidable role of businessman to create a band of loyal customers who ask for credit. It is a *sine-qua-non* for the very survival of any business entity. In this background credit is deemed to hold a position of high esteem in the business arena.

Hence, giving credit is a continuous character and associated responsibility rather than a course of selling goods on credit and keeping contact with customers of varied nature, temperament, tenacity and credere.

Of course, as human beings the customers are endowed with different degrees of nature namely character, capacity and capital. In other words a sense of reliance, answer balances and financial soundness should always have their due consideration. Otherwise collection of dues will be highly problematic. One should not be charitable or philanthropic because his position will become perilous. He should strike a balance and follow the policy of flexibility to remain in business, to regain the customers, to rejuvenate the position and to regulate his own business.

Some customers may be (a) Sincere (b) loyal (c) honest (d) regular in repayment. But some customers may be (d) cunning (e) deceitful (f) repugnant (g) niggardly (h) or almost bankrupt.

Therefore, collection of ledger account balances due from individuals and institutions, presents a series of impediments, and prolific communication alone may be the course of action.

The general position of inference may be summed up as follows:

(a) Some have and pay.

(b) Some have but do not want to pay.

(c) Some do not have and fail to pay.

(d) Some may appear to have but in reality they are on the verge of insolvency in their financial affairs.

In some cases, apparently any resort by seller to the legal course of action may prove to be a futile job. Hence, credit collection is not an easy joke. Therefore, the procedure suggested below will have to be adopted for human persuasion, reminding, demanding, and then receiving or lawfully penalising the cheating cases.

Collection letters are also named as "DUNNING LETTERS". It refers to a series of letters written repeatedly to remind him to pay cash and settle the accounts.

Collection Methods: Telephone calls, personal visits, correspondence, telegram and sending drafts.

Collection Routine: It refers to normal procedure necessary for the collection of accounts. Here, the stages include -

1. Sending a copy of statement of account indicating the due date.
2. A brief letter with second copy of statement of account presuming that either it has not reached or has been over looked by him.
3. Asking for payment of debt in a firm and polite way within a fixed date.
4. A final appeal to pay or with a sense of argument to clear off the debt or face the law.

Hints on writing collection letters:

1. Be sympathetic but rigid (use tact and skill).
2. Do not use grudging expression - use an amicable expression.
3. Provide timely advice with points to overcome business crisis (be resourceful).
4. Prick his conscience.
5. Pinpoint self-interest.
6. Hit at his psychology.
7. Remark his behaviour.
8. Try to retain customer by eliciting information, reading his mind and taking stock of the situation.

Replies to Collection Letters : Some Hints:

Many a times a trader may be in a precarious condition quite ineffable and unbearable. Trade depression attributable to unsatisfactory sales might have made his business vicious. Be it any reason for his incapacity to settle the accounts, there should be free and frank admission of truthful position. He may seek extension of time for payment or solicit the seller to grant him permission for payment by installments. Chiefly he should be a man of reality, backed by desire to pay the debt at least as when his financial position improves. As a debtor he might also be a trader but he should acknowledge the sympathy revealed by the seller in his dealings. Eventually, it may be said escapism and deceitful attitude. Prolonging to save his skin or devouring the property of a sincere seller or living at the cost of helpless creditor especially in absence of should be buried with a sense of human approach to the problem. This will avoid unwarranted plethora of communication to light the lamp of sincerity in the minds of traders as debtors or creditors as the case may be.

Other Collection Methods Include the Following:

1. *Telephone Call:* All the customers may not have telephone facility. Hence, difficult to inform them over phone. Local customers may be easily contacted. The greater the distance, the greater is the impedient for immediate information. Moreover, the lesser the amount, the more of superfluous nature, it becomes, so far as calls and remainders are concerned.

2. *Personal Call:* The relevance of personal contact is always high, but, many customers may not be that plain enough to contact and agree to pay. In case of large scale business, since the number of customers may be limited, giving a chance to the buyer to appear before the creditor may produce more effect in timely collection.

3. *Telegram:* It is widely followed in the United States. It easily catches the attention of the customer and compels the client to contact the creditor. Owing to drawal of rapt attention, rapid response and prompt action, this method is admittedly of avail.

4. *Bill of Exchange:* When a customer is long overdue, many a time the business house may draw a demand bill or payable at sight for the balance not yet settled. The seller will send the bill for collection through his banker, the matter will certainly be brought to the notice of the customer and thus, he will be constrained to think of paying off and settling the amount due to him. Refusal of written instrument of negotiation for a flimsy cause, will bring discredit to the buyer as a debtor. Every debtor is basically bothered of retaining his status in the commercial circles, hence, he will be forced to honour the bill.

5. *The Protection:* Certain societies for trade protection function both in the United Kingdom and the United States to assist the merchants in enabling them to collect the dues from purchasers. In case of non-availability, evasion, avoidance, deceitful behaviour and no response at all, of the debtor, the details about the debtor will be supplied by the seller. Now, the department will address the letters normally worded with a sense of politeness to the buyer to repay the debt. If the debtor keeps mum, the Trade Protection Society will mention in its report the debtor's name as being bad in repayment. Both the members and outside public will be much affected;

certainly the buyer's entity in business will be at stake. Thus, at least with an apprehension of facing ill repute, the debtor will try to repay the debt and settle the account.

6. *Correspondence:* When deals are put in black and white, it affords us a documentary evidence. Such a record will be both permanent and confidential. Knowledge of contents in a letter will be confined to only two corespondents- the writer and the receiver of it. Mere posting a letter will work out cheaper than face-to-face talk between the creditor and the buyer.

COLLECTION SERIES (FROM LETTERS)

I. FIRST LETTER (A Statement of Account enclosed)

SOWRABHA WATCH COMPANY

22, Puspak Road,
Market Circle, Tumkur - 2
1st June 2006

THE KARAWAK TRADING CO.,
Aruna Vriththa, Koratagere -4.

Dear Sir,

As on 31st May, 206, on glancing through the ledger accounts, we noticed that your balance due to us is Rs. 6,00,000.00/- (Six lakhs only) only. A statement of Account is enclosed to this letter.

If you could remit the settlement of your account, we would very much appreciate it.

Yours faithfully,
For Sowrabha Watch Co.,
R. Narayanan, Manager

II. SECOND LETTER (Statement of Account)

Statement of Account

SOWRABHA WATCH COMPANY

22, Puspak Road, Market Circle, Tumkur -2

1st June, 2006

THE KARARWAK TRADING CO.,
Aruna Vriththa,
Koratagere -4

DR. TO SOWRABHA WATCH CO.,

Terms : 3 ¼ % 1 month

2006		**Rs.**	**Rs.**
May 1	To Balance b/d		50,000.00
May 2	By Cash	50,000.00	

May 9	To Goods Sold	1,50,000.00	
May 19	To Goods Sold	1,50,000.00	
May 22	By Cash	50,000.00	1,00,000.00
May 24	To Goods Sold	3,50,000.00	7,00,000.00
			6,00,000.00

E. &. O. E.

Your Early Payment is appreciated.

R. Narayanan,

Manager.

III. SECOND LETTER WITH A DUPLICATE STATEMENT OF ACCOUNT ENCLOSED

SOWRABHA WATCH COMPANY

22, Puspak Road,

Market Circle, Tumkur -2

25th June 2006

THE KARARWAK TRADING CO.,

Aruna Vriththa,

Koratagere -4.

Dear Sir,

Re: Settlement of Account No. RL/4321

We brought to your attention the unpaid amount as per your Account with us bearing no. STC/420/dt. 16th January, 2006 of Rs. 6,00,000/-. Uptill now, no response at all from you. May we presume that our message must have missed your perusal. Hence, a duplicate statement of Account enclosure for your reference and early settlement.

Yours faithfully,

For Sowrabha Watch Co.,

R. Narayanan,

Manager.

IV. THIRD LETTER WITH A STIPULATED DATE FOR SETTLEMENT

SOWRABHA WATCH COMPANY

22, Puspak Road,
Market Circle, Tumkur -2
18th June, 2006

THE KARARWAK TRADING CO.,
Aruna Vriththa,
Koratagere - 4.

Dear Sir,

Re: Settlement of Account No. RL/4321

We are upset to note that you have conveniently brushed aside the letters, we wrote you hither to, on 1st and 16th June, 2006.

As the Account is outstanding for long, we demand of you to clear it off, latest by 15th August, 2006.

Yours faithfully,
For Sowrabha Watch Co.,
R. Narayanan
(Manager)

V. FOURTH LETTER - PAYMENT DEMANDED AND DRAFT EXPECTED

SOWRABHA WATCH COMPANY

22, Puspak Road,
Market Circle, Tumkur - 2
25th June, 2006

THE KARARWAK TRADING CO.,
Aruna Vriththa,
Koratagere -4.

Dear Sir,

Re: Settlement of Account RL/4321

So far, no reply from you nor any mode of settlement at all. You have neglected our previous letters of 1st and 16th June, 2006. Term of credit expired long before we lettered you first for remittance.

Even now you have to pay us in full on your account with us on 15th Aug, 2006; or else, we will expect you to sign our Bill at sight.

"Be the reaper of Credit; never be the eraser of credence".

Yours faithfully,
For Sowrabha Watch Co.,
R. Narayanan (Manager).

VI. FOURTH LETTER - Warning Debtor of your Approaching Solicitor.

SOWRABHA WATCH COMPANY

22, Puspak Road,
Market Circle, Tumkur - 2
16th Aug. 2006

THE KARARWAK TRADING CO.,
Aruna Vriththa, Koratagere - 4.

Dear Sir,

Re: Settlement of Account RL/4321

We sent you repeatedly the statement of account due from you date-wise but, all that is now proved futile.

Therefore, now you take note of our decision to hand over the file, in your name for further legal course of action, to the solicitor, if you don't care for settlement of your account with us on or before 10th Sept. 2006.

Yours faithfully,
For Sowrabha Watch Co.,
R. Narayanan
(Manager)

VII. FOURTH LETTER - Bill Dishonoured and hence, lawful resort- advice needed.

SOWRABHA WATCH COMPANY

22, Puspak Road,
Market Circle, Tumkur -2
16th Aug. 2006

THE KARARWAK TRADING CO.,
Aruna Vriththa,
Koratagere-4.

Dear Sir,

Re: Settlement of account RL/4321

We are hurt by your refusal to make payment of the bill accepted on 11th July, 2006. Thus, we insist on your paying us the balance immediately.

If you fail to pay the balance due on or before 10th Sept. 2006, we will request our solicitor to deal with you in any fashion the law may direct for receiving the overdue amount.

Don't be shareholder of displeasure.

Yours faithfully,
For Sowrabha Watch Co.,
R. Narayanan (Manager)

VIII. FOURTH LETTER - Reply to letter No. 4 (in series III Letter) with a stipulated date for settlement

THE KARARWAK TRADING COMPANY

Aruna Vrithha, Koratagere-4.
17th August 2006

SOWRABHA WATCH COMPANY
22, Puspak Road, Market Circle,
Tumkur-2.

Dear Sir,

We got your letter of 31st July, 2006 asking for immediate clearance of balance on account.

We feel sorry to inform you that the watches do not have much demand now. Nearly 50% of your consignment is still with us. Market is now a bit dull. I seek extension of time limit to expect the settlement of account with you at least by 3 months.

I hope you will grant my request.

Yours faithfully,
For The Kararwak Trading Co.,
K. Nambike Murthy

IX. Reply to Letter No. 8 Asking for Acceptance of Bill

SOWRABHA WATCH COMPANY

22, Puspak Road,
Market. Circle, Tumkur -2
20th Aug 2006

THE KARARWAK TRADING CO.,
Aruna Vriththa
Koratagere -4.

Dear Sir,

In the light of the explanation you have tendered us in your letter of 17th August, 2006. We permit you to settle the balance due to us at a later date. Now, we demand you to give your acceptance to the Bill sent along with this. The Bill will be due for being honoured on 1st Dec, 2006.

We hope you will meet the Bill on the due date.

Yours faithfully,
For Sowrabha Watch Co.,
C. Ghanandaari and Sons.
Proprietors.

X. LETTER REGARDING ACCOUNT SETTLEMENT

THE KARARWAK TRADING COMAPNY

Aruna Vriththa
Koratagere -4
4th Dec. 2006

SOWRABHA WATCH COMPANY
22, Puspak Road,
Market Cricle, Tumkur -2.

Dear Sir,

We feel sorry to state that we could not reply soon to your earlier letters. A slight change in the accounts section staff duties resulted in this delay. Now, we are sending you a draft for Rs. 6,00,000/- towards our account settlement.

We hope that this delayed settlement will not be viewed as our incapacity to meet the obligation on the due date.

Yours faithfully,
For The Karawak Trading Co.,
V. Sathyavan.

XI. INTIMATING A CUSTOMER TO AVAIL OF CASH DISCOUNT

SOUTH CENTRAL SOAP WORKS CO.,

Stella Mary Road,
Malleswaram, Bangalore-3
18th Jan. 2006.

M/S. GANDHARVA SOAP STALLS
Fragrance Street,
Sandal Town, Tumkur -2.

Dear Sir,

You have been our customer for nearly two decades, you have always reaped the benefit of discount of 2%. Your account is long due. In case you pay it before the end of this month, you will be eligible for taking advantage of it. This only reminds you of such a feasibility. We wish that you will settle the account in time.

Yours faithfully,
For South Central Soap Works Co.,
M.K. Nijaswaroop.

BANK CORRESPONDENCE

One of the very essential organs of commerce is a banking institution. Bank plays a vital role in smoothening the business operations. Not only in the business, but also in the life of most persons, bank is an important institution. But, for a business it is an essential institution as large amounts of money required for business flow from this financial institution. Most of the business transactions today are of credit nature and banks help in running such credit business through the negotiable and other instruments. Banks discharge various types of functions like accepting deposits, advancing money, rendering agency services and various other miscellaneous functions. Particularly in 1980s, the whole complexion of bank has changed and banks have entered the new areas of operations like housing finance, Mutual Fund business, issuing Commercial Papers, etc. They have come out from their shells of traditional banking and have started operating in many new areas which are opposed to traditional banking system. We can list here the functions of a commercial bank.

I. **Primary Functions**:

(i) Accepting Deposits

(ii) Granting Loans

II. **Subsidiary Functions**:

(i) Issuing letter of credit

(ii) Accepting and collecting the bills on behalf of customers

(iii) Discharging various types of miscellaneous functions like acting as agents of customers, acting as custodian of valuables of customers, issuing the travellers cheques, discounting the bills, supplying status enquiry information to another bank which is needed by customer, acting as executors, advising the customer on investments etc.

These different types of functions of banks have necessitated to write afferent types of letters both from customers and banks. The correspondence may be between the banks or between the banker and customer or between head office and branch or between the bank and government. It is a tough job particularly for customers to write precise letters. Letters need clarity, courtesy, and communicable language. Tact and secrecy too, are of great importance, especially when replying in the negative. As the commodity dealt is money, there must be complete trust between the two parties writing letters.

Drafting a bank letter needs much skill and patience. Banks are governed by rules and regulations. Many banking operations are not known by the general public. Therefore, the authority of a bank (Manager) has the responsibility of educating the public regarding bank operations and also instruct them to utilise the various services rendered by banks. Hence, the bank correspondence varies from operation to operation and customer to customer. In such a situation, the style, the tone of the letter, the matter, etc., varies from letter to letter.

Due to the fast changing economic life of the country, Reserve Bank of India- the monetary authority of the country- will be issuing various new regulations from time to time catering to the needs of the economy. There will be changes in lending policy, interest rates, new types of loans to be granted, various types of savings and investment policies, etc. All these changes have to be brought to the notice of customers. Hence wide variety of letters have to be drafted. In this chapter an attempt has been made to show some of the important specimen letters to make the reader have an acquaintance with these letters.

As stated in the earlier paragraphs, the bank correspondence can be of four types:

(1) between banker and customer.

(2) between banks.

(3) between the bank and the government.

(4) between head office and the branch.

1. Correspondence Between Banker and Customers

There are very many types of letters exchanged between the banker and customer. It may relate to opening of an account, or relating to advances or relating to various types of agency services rendered to the customers. We have brought out here some of the letters for the understanding of our readers.

Specimen - 1: Opening of Bank Account

This is a letter written by a prospective customer to a banker. The prospect may be an individual, a firm, a body corporate or a co-operative enterprise. Whoever may be the person that writes, the sum and substance of the letter is same. But in case of firms all the partners have to sign the letter and submit a copy of Partnership Deed for examination by the banker and in case of Corporate enterprises, the Articles of Association and Memorandum of Association have to be submitted. The authorised signatories to the letter have to sign the letter.

A resolution copy permitting the company to open the bank account should also be sent. The letter must be crisp and unwanted points are to be avoided.

RASHMI ENTERPRISES LTD.

No. 25, 6th main, 5th cross,
Malleswaram, Bangalore - 560 003.
Ph.22348520
Date: Jan 3rd 2006

The Manager,
Karnataka Bank Ltd.,
Malleswaram, Bangalore- 560 003.

Sir,

Our firm wishes to open a current account with you. We are submitting here in duly filled application form along with the Deed of our firm.

Sri. Vijaya Bhaskar, Proprietor, General Hardware Stores, Malleswaram, Bangalore, an account holder of your bank has given the introduction letter, which is also enclosed.

We are depositing Rs. 5,000 as initial deposit. It is sent in cash with our assistant Sri. Ganesh. Please accept the deposit and open a current account in our firm's name. Sri. Bharath Ram, our

Managing Partner is authorised to operate the said account. A copy of the resolution to this effect has also been enclosed.

Please send (i) a cheque book (ii) a pass book (iii) a pay-in-slip book to operate the proposed account.

Assuring you of our best co-operation.

Yours faithfully,
(Sd) Bharath Ram,
Bhargava Ram,
Partners

Encl.

1. Introduction letter from Vijaya Bhaskar
2. Partnership Deed
3. Resolution copy authorising Bharath Ram to operate the Account.

Specimen - 2: Request to Stop Payment.

The customer requested his banker to stop payment regarding a cheque already issued to a third party. The reason may be that the cheque might have lost in transit or it may be due the overpayment against the customer's account or for any other reason. In such a situation an appropriate letter has to be sent to the banker. Following is the specimen which can be considered as a guide.

RATAN ENTERPRISES

No. 5, College Road,
Gulbarga.
Dt: 15th Feb. 2006

The Manager,
State Bank of Mysore,
Gulbarga.

Dear Sir,

This letter is in continuation of the Telegram we sent earlier, which reads as follows:

Stop Payment Cheque No. 867510 Dated 10th Feb. 2006 for Rupees One Lakh. Payee Mayappa Bros. We have been informed that the said Cheque No. 867510 has been lost in transit.

We request you to issue the necessary instructions to stop payment on the cheque.

Yours faithfully,
(Sd) RATAN
For Ratan Enterprises.

Specimen - 3: Reply to the above letter.

The reply may be positive or negative. If the information for stop payment has been sent in time the banker will be obliged to stop payment. If it is received late, the account by that time might have been debited. Hence, he is bound to send a negative reply. Following specimen gives a positive reply.

STATE BANK OF MYSORE

Gulbarga.
Ph:2542628
16th Feb. 2006

Mr. Ratan,
Ratan Enterprises,
No. 5, College Road,
Gulbarga.

Dear Sir,

Re: Request to Stop payment

We are in receipt of your telegram and your letter confirming your telegram on 15th Feb. 2006, requesting us to stop payment on cheque number 867510 dated 10th Feb. 2006 for Rs. One lakh drawn in favour of Sri Mayappa Bros.

Immediately on the receipt of your letter, we have issued necessary instructions to our staff to stop payment on that cheque. Please note that the bank does not hold itself responsible, if payment is made on the cheque by oversight or because of pressure of business.

Yours faithfully,
(Sd) H.S. Raja Rao,
Senior Manager,
SBM

Specimen - 4: Advice on overdrawing the Account

This letter intimates the customer that his account has been overdrawn. Bank also informs that without prior arrangement, such overdrawing cannot be allowed in future. These are the two points to be stressed in such letter. Observe the following specimen:

STATE BANK OF INDIA

Singri Complex, TIPTUR
3rd Feb. 2006

Sri. Nagaraja Rao,
Doddapet, TIPTUR.

Sir,

Ref: Your overdrawn Account

I wish to bring to your kind notice that, as a result of payment today on your cheque Rs. 20,000, your account is overdrawn to the extent of Rs. 15,000.

Please note that it is not the practice of the bank to honour cheques drawn in excess of the balance of the customer's account, unless specific arrangements have been made for overdraft facilities.

I have, of course, unhesitatingly honoured your cheque. But in future, if you require to overdraw your account, I would request you to make arrangements for overdraft with the bank. Such an arrangement would remove any possibility of your cheques being dishonoured on grounds of insufficient funds. Otherwise, please arrange to verify the balance before the cheques are issued.

Yours faithfully,
(Sd) Bharathan.
Manager, SBI.

Specimen - 5: Reply to customer's complaint

In this letter, bank expresses regret for intimating the overdrawing account and also requests the customer to keep sufficient balance in the account to honour cheques.

VIJAYA BANK

Malleswaram Branch,
Bangalore - 560 003.
Dated : 3rd March 2006

Sri Ravirajan,
No. 15, 8th Cross,
Malleswaram, Bangalore - 560 003.

Sir,

Ref: Complaint dated 25th Feb. 2006

We are in receipt of your letter dated 25th Feb. 2006. We regret to note that you have been very much embarrassed to know that your account (number 4695) with us has been overdrawn.

However, we would like to bring to your notice that you have issued two more cheques for Rs.15,000 and Rs. 20,000 respectively against the said account. As a result, your account stands overdrawn to the extent of Rs.10,000.

Although we regret for the inconvenience caused to you, we shall appreciate, if you place sufficient funds in your account to meet such contingencies.

Yours faithfully,
S.R. Raghuveer,
Branch Manager.

Specimen - 6: Loans and Overdrafts

Loans and overdrafts are the earning assets of commercial banks. Banks grant loans and overdrafts to different types of customers considering the security offered, solvency of the customer. The term of the loan and the type of business carried on by the prospective customer. The advance may be to priority sector, or to the self-employed people or to the business firms or to the general public. The purpose are different in each and loans to each category are governed by certain rules and regulations. The interest rates also vary.

The security, banks would like to accept, should have liquidity nature. They should be capable of being readily converted into cash. Fixed assets are not normally accepted as security, because of difficulties of assessment and complications arising from varied systems of ownership and rules of succession. Validity of title is also difficult to ascertain. But the corporate securities, life insurance policies and non-perishable goods are accepted as security.

Keeping these aspects in view, banks write only short letters and tell the customer, whether his proposal to avail loan can be accepted or not. If their lending policies do not permit them to sanction loan, they say that they cannot accommodate. However, banks educate the customer giving him the proper direction to avail the loan. Following are some of the specimens of such letters.

EVERGREEN BANK LTD.

No.I, Sathya Dev Road,
Sharadanagar
Dt: 27th Dec. 2005

Sri. Ranjan Das,
Messers. Sathyapal & Co.,
Naveen Building, Laxmi Extension,
Sharadanagar.

Sir,

We are in receipt of your letter requesting for a loan of Rs.50,00,000=00 to carry out the activities of your firm. You have offered your office building and the shares held by one of your partners as the security for the proposed loan.

We are very pleased to sanction the requested sum. But the security you have offered is not acceptable. The bank can advance loan against the company shares only when they stand in the name of the firm and not in the name of the individual partner. Besides this, the acceptability of the share depends upon the market price and the image of that company in the capital market.

The building you have offered is in a bad shape and situated in a locality where it cannot be easily disposed. Therefore, it can cover only 25% of the loan asked.

In view of these facts, we request you to provide adequate security for the loan asked for. Please submit also the following documents.

1. Partnership Deed.
2. Audited Balance Sheet for the past two years.
3. Acceptance of all partners, authorising you to handle the loan deal.
4. Details of the scheme for which the loan is sought.

We are pleased to consider your loan proposal positively on the receipt of said information, documents and acceptable securities from you.

Yours faithfully,
(Sd) Sathyanath (Manager).

Specimen - 7: Issue of Drafts

The banks will be regularly issuing drafts to its customers. To secure a bank draft, the customer will have to request the bank to issue the same, stating the amount, place where it should be paid, the name and address of the recipient etc., The banks have a specific printed form to issue a draft. It has to be filled and signed by the person who sends money. However, a specimen letter to this effect has been produced below.

VASANT ENTERPRISES

No.5, I main, Gandhinagar,
Bangalore - 560 009.
13th Jan. 2006.

The Manager
Rashmi Bank Ltd.,
Gandhinagar
Bangalore - 560 009.

Sir,

I am in need of a Bank Draft for Rs.5,000 payable at Tiptur. Kindly issue the same.

Payable to :
M/s. Mohan Service Centre
K.R. Extension
TIPTUR - 572 202.

Thanking You.

Yours truly,
(sd./-) Vasanth.
For Vasanth Enterprises.

ISSUE OF LETTERS OF CREDIT

Letters of Credit is an introduction letter given by the banker or by the individuals to far off persons or banks, recommending to give a specified sum of money at the request of the bearer of the instrument. The specified amount will be paid to the holder of the letter of credit on proof of identity and signature. Here we have considered only letters of credit issued by bankers.

Letters of credit issued by banks are used by business people in international as well as national trade. When businessmen are on tour and when they require huge amount of money to complete business deals, they make use of the letter of credit as they cannot carry large amount with them. Traveller's cheques can be used only if it is required. In case of traveller's cheques, the money has to be first deposited with the banker. But in this case, there is no such deposit of money, only the instrument will be issued by the banker, accepting the responsibility of clearing the obligation of the customer of the bank who is on tour. He can use the instrument in times of need.

These letters of credit are addressed to the specific persons or banks at definite places where the recommended travelling businessman can encash such letters and complete their business deals. This is an instrument issued by the banker requesting the addressee to pay the specific sum to the recommended person.

Letters of credit may be :

(i) Commercial

(ii) Non-commercial

Commercial letters of credit are issued by banks to conduct the business operations of their customers, national or international. These will be prepared in a set form, but they differ in sum and substance.

Non-commercial letters of credit are issued by the bank to a traveller, asking their branches or authorised agents to give a specified sum of money at the said destination, which will be guaranteed by it.

Letters of credit may be simple letter of credit (issued to only one person) or circular letter of credit (issued to many persons concerned).

Letter of credit normally contains the following points:

1. The name and address of the person to whom it is addressed.
2. The name and address of the recipient.
3. The specimen signature of the recipient. This can be taken on a separate card and along with the L/C.
4. Formal introduction of the recipient and his purpose of tour.
5. The time period for which it is valid.

6. The sum to be paid.
7. The mode of repayment by the issuing banker.
8. Other special instructions, if any.

Following is the specimen Letter of Credit issued by bankers.

Specimen - 8: Circular Letter of Credit :

LAKSHMI BANK LTD.

No.5, Avenue Road,
Bangalore - 560 002.
2nd April. 2006.

LETTER OF CREDIT

No.41356 Amount Rs. 10,00,000=00

Valid upto 15th October 2006

Dear Sir,

We have the pleasure in introducing Mr. Srinath, Area Representative of Rashmi Pharmaceuticals of Chennai, who has been our esteemed customer for the past 10 years. He is visiting Maharashtra, Andhra Pradesh and Orissa at the behest of his head office to explore the possibilities of marketing of their products in these states and to enter into contracts with the dealers of these territories, if the terms and conditions of the firm are agreeable to them.

We request you to provide him with the required funds upto Rs. 10,00,000/- (Rupees Ten Lakhs only) against the sight drafts, drawn on this office. The prevailing rates may please be charged by you at the time of drawing these drafts. Please note that each draft you issue should be clearly marked with the number of L/C 41356. The draft should also contain the signature as shown in the separate letter of indication enclosed herein bearing the same number.

This letter of credit is valid upto 15th October 2006 and all drafts drawn during this period will be honoured by us.

We also request you to mark on the back of this L/C the amount for which each draft is drawn and enclose this letter duly cancelled after issuing the last draft.

Yours sincerely,
(Sd/-) Manager
Lakshmi Bank Ltd.

On the back of the letter

Addresses to whom the L/Cs are issued should be given.

1. Manager, Bank of Maharashtra, Pune.

2. Manager, Bank of India, Karad.
3. Manager, Bank of Sourashtra, Fort Mumbai.
4. Manager, Bank of Miraj, Miraj.
5. Manager, Bank of Orissa, Bhuvaneshwar.
6. Manager, Bank of Hyderabad, Hyderabad.
7. Manager, Bank of Karur, Guntur A.P.

Details of payment

Date	The name of the recipient	Amount Paid (Figures) (in words)

Annexure 1: Letter showing specimen signature

(This is also called Letter of Indication)

LAKSHMI BANK LTD.

Bangalore - 560 002.

No : 41356 Date : 15-7-2006

To Messrs,

1.

2.

3.

4.

5.

6.

7.

Dear sir,

Sri Srinath to whom this letter of credit bearing No.41356 has been issued, has his signature as follows.

....

(Specimen Signature)

Yours sincerely,

(Sd/-) Manager.

PS. This letter has to be returned

Cash Credit Accounts (cc)

Cash Credit accounts (cc) are generally referred to as "CC" accounts in banking circles. As the very name indicates, these accounts provide credit to the customer on the security of stocks of raw materials, packing materials and finished goods held by the customer. In other words, the stocks are said to have been 'charged' in favour of the bank. Again some or all of these stocks may lie in the custody of the banker (in which case the facility is called "Closed CC") or the customer may be have free access to these stocks (in which case the facility is called "Open CC").

The amount of loan released to the customer depends on the value of the stocks held by the customer. Depending on whether the stocks held are raw materials or packing materials or finished goods, the bank may release 60 to 75% of the value of the stocks by way of loan. To calculate the loanable funds, the customer is required to submit 'Stock Statements' periodically to the bank. If the loan outstanding against the customer exceeds the stipulated 60 to 75% of the value of the stocks, the customer is required to pay up immediately the amount drawn in excess. During the currency of the account, the banker is free to inspect the stocks lying with the customer to check the veracity of the information furnished in the stock statements submitted periodically to the bank by the customer. The duration of the loan account is generally three years. Upon expiry of the said period, the banker may renew it for a further period having regard to the creditworthiness of the borrower.

Specimen-9: The following is a letter addressed by ABC Limited, Mumbai to State Bank of India, Churchgate Branch, Mumbai, seeking a CC limit of Rs. 25,00,000.

ABC LIMITED
"El Dorado" # 521, F.M. Road, Fort,
Mumbai: 400 001.

Tel: 022-2354 5648
SBI/CC/567 April 25th 2006.
The Manager, State Bank of India,
Churchgate Branch, Mumbai: 400 001.

Dear Sir,

Sub: Cash Credit limit of Rs. 25 lakhs

Further to the discussions our Mr. Trehan had with you on the subject, we enclose the following for your perusal:

1. Application for sanction of Cash Credit limit of Rs. 25 lakhs, duly filled in and signed.
2. Certified copy of Board Resolution requesting the bank to sanction the CC limit.
3. Copies of our audited Final Accounts for the past five years.
4. Profitability Statement of our company.

5. Projected Balance Sheets for the next five years.
6. Statement of stocks held by us as of date in our various godowns and depots.
7. List of agencies we hold, together with copies of contracts we have with them.

We are agreeable to hypothecate our stocks and charge our book debts in favour of the bank. We are agreeable too, to furnish the personal guarantee of three of our directors. We would only be too glad to furnish such other information, as you may need.

We request you to sanction our proposal at the earliest.

Thank you,
Yours truly,
For ABC Limited
(Goutham Aradhya),
Authorised Signatory

***Specimen - 10*: Request for overdraft Facility**

MADHU ELECTRONICS LTD.,
No. 5, Industrial Estates,
Rajajinagar, Bangalore - 10.

The Manager,
Canara Bank,
Rajajinagar,
Bangalore – 10

May 15th, 2006

Sir,

Ref : Overdraft limit for Rs. 5 lakhs.

In continuation of our discussion with you last week, we apply for an overdraft limit for Rs. 5 lakhs.

The following documents are enclosed for your consideration:

1. The list of Directors, together with the details of companies, firms, etc., in which they are interested.
2. Audited Balance Sheets for the last three years.
3. An inventory statement showing the stock held as on today.
4. Projected balance sheets for the next 5 years.
5. Projected cash flow statement for the next five years.
6. A profit statement as required in your form.
7. A list of agencies that we hold, together with copies of contracts with them.

We are pleased to furnish any other information required by you.

We are prepared to hypothecate our stocks and accounts receivable to you, maintaining a 40% margin. We also offer the personal guarantee of two of our directors as additional security.

Please expedite the examination of this proposal and call us at your convenience for any other required information and for the inspection of our depots and godowns.

Yours faithfully,
For Madhu Electronics,
H.S. Govind,
Secretary.

Specimen - 11: Sanction letter from the Bank

This letter contains the sanction accorded to the customer. It may also contain the rules and regulations to be followed by the customer while operating the current account. The letter may also contain a demand for additional security.

CANARA BANK
Rajajinagar,
Bangalore -560 010.

May 20th 2006

The Secretary,
Madhu Electronics,
Rajajinagar,
Bangalore - 10.

Sir,

We have examined your overdraft proposal for Rs.5 lakhs. We are pleased to sanction the overdraft of Rs. 4 lakhs subject to the following conditions.

1. The security offered by you is inadequate to cover the sanctioned limit. Therefore, you have to furnish additional security of stock or approved corporate securities you have, if any.
2. Clean maintenance of overdraft account is a must.
3. The bank holds the right of withdrawing the facility at any time.

Yours faithfully,
(sd) Manager,
Canara Bank.

Specimen - 12: Cancelling the overdraft account

BANK OF INDIA
Basavanagudi Branch
Bangalore - 560 004.

Tel. No. 605470 July 1, 2006

The Manager,
Rashmi Electronics,
Basavangudi.

Sir,

The overdraft of Rs. 5,00,000=00 sanctioned to you in last January has not been used by you even once. Now, we feel justified in withdrawing this facility from 1st Aug. 2006. We are forced to take this decision as the facility granted to you locks up our funds unnecessarily.

However, we assure you to sanction the facility any time you need in future. Please collect your securities deposited with the bank against the O/D facility.

Yours truly,
(Sd) Branch Manager.

Specimen-13: The following is a letter addressed by XYZ Ltd, New Delhi to the State Bank of Bikaner & Jaipur, asking the latter to open a Current Account.

XYZ LIMITED
Anupam Complex, Saket,
NEW DELHI: 110 017

Tel: 011-2651 8754 Jan 20th.2006.

SBBJ/CA/323
The Manager,
State Bank of Bikaner & Jaipur,
Anupam Complex, Saket,
NEW DELHI: 110 017.

Dear Sir,

Re: Opening a Current Account with you.

This letter is to request you to open a current account in your bank in the name of our company. Towards this end, we furnish the following:

1. Application for opening the Current Account duly filled in and signed.

2. Memorandum and Articles of Association of the company.
3. Certified copy of Board Resolution requesting the bank to open the current account.

We also request you to let us have a cheque book and Pay-in slips to enable us to transact with the bank.

Thank you,

Yours truly,
For XYZ Limited,
(Sridhar Honnalli),
Authorised Signatory.

INSURANCE CORRESPONDENCE

Insurance is a contract between two parties viz., the insured and the insurer. The insurer agrees to indemnify the insured in the event of loss. Of course, this benefit accrues to the insured at a price, called premium. Thus, premium is the consideration paid by the insured to the insurer for this protection. Insurance is also called professional risk since the insurer undertakes to make good, wholly or partially, the loss incurred by many insured parties. Quite simply, many parties share the risk in insurance.

Obviously, the risk that a party has to take if he is not insured is heavy. He and he alone is responsible for the damage or loss, that may occur. But if the party insures his risk, his loss is minimised because the insurer has to indemnify him, in accordance with the provisions of the insurance policy. However, save life insurance, no money is returned to the insured unless he has incurred a loss. Thus, insurance cannot be taken for the purpose of making any profit but only as a safeguard against loss. Naturally, a contract of insurance revolves around three basic principles, viz., utmost good faith, indemnity and insurable interest.

Utmost good faith: When a contract of insurance is entered into, the insured has to furnish all the information in order to decide whether the risk being covered is a good risk or a bad risk. It is imperative to follow the principle of 'utmost good faith'.

Indemnity: The indemnity principle ensures that insurance does not become a device for earning profits. The insurer undertakes to indemnify only to the extent of actual loss. In other words, indemnity will be paid only on the actual price of goods. Effectively, over-insurance or under-insurance is ruled out by the indemnity principle.

To illustrate, if goods worth Rs.4,00,000 are insured for Rs. 7,00,000, in the event of total loss, the insured will be indemnified only to the extent of Rs.4,00,000. On the other hand, if goods worth Rs.7,00,000 are insured for only Rs.4,00,000, the insured will be indemnified only to the extent of Rs. 4,00,000.

Insurable Interest: The insured must have an insurable interest in the goods that he is insuring. This means that the loss or destruction of the goods should harm the insured and the insured should stand to benefit as long as the goods are safe. In the absence of insurable interest, people may insure goods belonging to other people (from which they should not derive any benefit), but may claim indemnity in the event of destruction of the said goods.

Life Insurance: This is a contract between the insured and the insurer, whereby the insurer agrees to pay a fixed amount after a certain period to the insured or in the case of his death, to his nominees, assigns or heirs. Indemnity does not arise in the case of life insurance. The insured keeps paying the premia till the policy matures. At the end of this period, the insured gets the amount he is insured for.

Marine Insurance: It covers loss incurred when goods are in transit, whether on land or ocean, between the warehouse of the origin of goods and the warehouse of their destination.

Fire Insurance: It is a contract wherein the insurer agrees to pay the agreed amount on specified goods to the insured if the goods are damaged by fire within a specified period. Unless there is a loss, the insured gets nothing, even though he has paid the premia.

The insurer inspects the goods to be insured and quotes the premium. Upon payment of the premium, the insured is issued a cover note stating that the policy is under preparation and the risk is covered from the date of issue of the cover note. When the policy is in force, any change in address must be immediately notified to the insurer. This is because such a change may call for an upward or downward modification of the premium, depending on whether the new address is a good or a bad risk. For instance, a Cracker factory beside a Mattress factory is a bad risk.

Specimen-1: Letter addressed to LIC of India, Bangalore, by Satish Sharma, requesting that his policy be henceforth serviced from Mumbai.

B/23, Jai Savitri,
Vallabh Baug Lane, Ghatkoper East,
Mumbai: 400 077,
April 19th, 2006.

The Manager,
LIC of India,
St. Marks Road, BANGALORE: 560 001.

Dear Sir,

Sub: Policy no: 856415478953

Effective April 23rd, 2006, my services have been transferred to Mumbai by my employer. Hence,

I would like my policy to be serviced by your branch at Fort, Mumbai, henceforth. Since my next premium falls due on the 21st of May, I would request you to do the needful in the matter at the earliest, under advice to your Fort, Mumbai branch.

Thanking you,

Yours truly,

(Satish Sharma)

cc to: LIC of India, F. M. Road, Fort, Mumbai-400001.

Specimen-2: Letter from Navin Shah seeking guidance from LIC of India, Ahmedabad, for lodging a claim consequent upon his father's death.

Gulmohar,
#13, Breshtwar Peth, Ahmedabad,
June 21, 2006

The Manager,
LIC of India,
Ellis Bridge, AHMEDABAD.

Dear Sir,

My father, Mr. Kishen Kant Shah expired on the 18th instant. He is survived by his wife, a son, the undersigned and two daughters, both married. I am single. He had insured his life with your branch under your policy no: 4573698541. The nominee is his wife.

In the circumstances, I request you to let us know the procedure to be followed to claim the sum insured.

Thanking you,

Yours truly,

(K. Navin Shah)

Specimen-3: Letter addressed by Swajay India Ltd, Mumbai, to New India Assurance Co. Ltd., Mumbai, seeking insurance cover on cotton bales in transit between Mumbai and Singapore.

SWAJAY INDIA LTD,
582, Garden Reach,
MUMBAI: 400 001
July 12, 2006

Tel: 033-25893211
NIACL/23/1
The New India Assurance Co Ltd,
M.G. Road,
MUMBAI - 400 001.

Dear Sir,

Please cover us for Rs.18,00,000=00 at 0.50 on cotton bales in transit between Mumbai and Singapore. The said bales are to be packed in the usual way and despatched by the vessel Dwaraka to the State Ware House in Singapore, where the bales will be collected by our consignee. It is to be understood clearly that the risk attaches immediately the goods leave our possession on the 15th July 2006.

Thank you,

Yours truly,
For Swajay India Ltd.
(R.K.Sondhi).
Authorised Signatory.

Specimen-4: Letter from Banerji & Banerji asking National Insurance Co. Ltd. Calcutta, to insure the plastic goods lying in their godown.

BANERJI & BANERJI

#231, Tollygunj,
KOLKOTA 500 026.
July 4, 2006

The Manager
The National Insurance Co Ltd,
324, Middleton Street,
KOLKUTTA: 700 001.

Dear Sir,

Subject: Issue Of Fire Policy

Please insure against fire the plastic goods of the value of Rs, 50,00,000=00 lying in our godown behind our office premises and issue a policy, covering the risk for a period of one year from today.

The Proposal Form, duly filled in and signed, is enclosed.

Thanking you,

Yours truly,
Banerji & Banerji,
(R.Keshtoo Mukerjee)
Authorised Signatory.

Specimen-5: Letter frorn Banerji & Banerji to their insurers intimating transfer of the insured plastic goods to a new godown.

BANERJI & BANERJI

#231, Tolly Gunj,
KOLKUTTA: 700 026.
July 14, 2006

REGISTERED MAIL

The Manager,
The National Insurance Co Ltd,
324, Middleton Street,
KOLKUTTA: 700 001.

Dear Sir,

Subject: FIRE POLICY no: 1079/06

The plastic goods covered by the subject Fire Policy will be transferred to Shed: 21, WBSSIDC Estate, Salt Lake City on the 22nd of this month. This is for your information.

We enclose the subject policy, which may please be returned to us after noting this fact.

Thanking you,

Yours truly,
For Banerji & Banerji,
(R.Keshtoo Mukerjee)
Authorised Signatory.

Enclosure (1)

Specimen-6: Banerji & Banerji write to the insurers after a huge fire destroy their insured goods. They also request the insurers to send them the relevant paper to claim loss and damage against the fire.

BANERJI & BANERJI

231, Tolly Gunj,
KOLKUTTA: 700 026.
July 14, 2006

The Manager,
The National Insurance Co Ltd,
324, Middleton Street, KOLKUTTA: 700 001.

Dear Sir,

Subject: FIRE POLICY no: 1079/06

We regret to inform you that the goods insured under the subject policy were destroyed in a massive fire that engulfed a large part of the WBSSIDC Estate last night. The authorities concerned are yet to ascertain the cause of the fire.

Approximately Rs. 50,00,000=00 lakhs worth of goods were lying in our godown at the time. Please send us the relevant papers by return of post to enable us prefer a claim.

Thanking you,

Yours truly,
For Banerji & Banerji
(R.Keshtoo Mukerjee)
Authorised Signatory.

Specimen-7: The insurer settles the claim.

The National Insurance Co. Ltd.

324, Middleton Street,
KOLKUTTA: 700 001.
July 29th 2006

BANERJI & BANERJI,
231, Tolly Gunj,
KOLKUTTA: 700 026.

Dear Sir,

Sub: Claim no: 131/06 under Policy No: 1079/06

We are in receipt of your fire claim for Rs. 50,00,000=00. Our surveyors, M/s, Bhimji & Co. inspected your godown on the 14th and submitted their report.

Accordingly, we are pleased to enclose our cheque no: 856221 of date on UCO Bank, Esplanade Branch, Calcutta, for Rs. 30,00,000=00 in full and final settlement of your claim. Please own receipt of the cheque.

Thanking you,

Yours truly,
for National Insurance Co Ltd,
(K.Sengupta).
Manager.

Specimen-8: Mr. Shivakumar writes to his insurer asking them to insure his motorcycle.

1588, 2nd Stage, 5th Main,
'E' Block, Rajajinagar,
BANGALORE: 560 010.

July 12th 2006

The Manager
The Oriental Insurance Co Ltd,
19th main, Rajajinagar,
BANGALORE: 560 010.

Dear Sir,

Subject: HERO HONDA MOTOR CYCLE-. KA-04 M-1456

I enclose-

1. Proposal Form duly filled in and signed
2. Copy of invoice covering the purchase of the subject motor cycle
3. Cheque no: 451366 of date on Dena Bank, Bangalore main branch for Rs. 525/- drawn in your favour

Please insure the subject vehicle comprehensively and let me have the policy at the earliest.

Thanking you,

Yours truly,
(S. Shivakumar)

1588, 2nd Stage, 5th Main,
'E' Block, Rajajinagar,
BANGALORE: 560 010.

July 3,2006

The Manager
The Oriental Insurance Co Ltd,
19th main, Rajajinagar,
BANGALORE- 560 010.

Dear Sir,

Subject: HERO HONDA MOTOR CYCLE: KA-04 M-1456

Motor Policy no 43691/06 covering the subject vehicle expires on July 11, 2006. I request you to renew the insurance for a further period of one year. I enclose cheque no. 491326 of date on Dena Bank, Bangalore main branch for Rs. 465/- drawn in your favour for the purpose.

Thanking you,

Yours truly,
(S. Shivakumar)

Telephones

Apart from the recent players like Tata, Reliance, BPL etc., in telecom sector, the department of Telecommunications of the Government of India provides telephone services to every nook and corner of our country. The Telecom network in the country has been divided into several Telecom Districts to ensure better administration. Each Telecom district covers several Exchanges in urban and/or rural areas. The Bangalore Telecom district for example, covers 81 Exchanges in the rural areas of Bangalore Revenue District, apart from covering suburban areas like Indiranagar, Jayanagar, Malleswaram, etc.

Telephone bills can be paid either in cash or by suitably drawn cheque or demand draft or through Electronic Clearing Services (ECS). Telephone bills are issued once in 2 months. Non-receipt of bills is not accepted as a reason for non-payment. Non-payment of bills will result in disconnection of the telephone.

Use Phonetic codes for better hearing

A – Army	J – Jam	S – Sister
B – Brother	K – King	T – Table
C – Cinema	L – Lady	U – Uncle
D – Doctor	M – Mother	V – Victory
E – English	N – Navy	W – Water
F – Father	O – Orange	X – X-ray
G – Gold	P – Paper	Y – Yellow
H – Hotel	Q – Queen	Z – Zebra
I – Indian	R – Raja	

Specimen-1: Mr. Dheeraj Bhargava registers for a new telephone connection by post.

#543, 19th Main, 11th Block,
Rajajinagar,
BANGALORE - 560 010.

July 24, 2005

REGISTERED MAIL

The Customer Service Centre (Malleswaram),
Swathi Complex,
BANGALORE: 560 020.

Dear Sir,

Subject: REGISTRATION FOR A NEW TELEPHONE CONNECTION

I wish to register for a new telephone connection under the General Scheme. Towards this end,

I enclose:

1. The prescribed application form, duly filled in and signed
2. Demand draft no: 2189/98 on Canara Bank, Townhall Branch, Bangalore for Rs. 2,000=00 in favour of RBI A/c AOTD, Bangalore (towards initial deposit).

Yours truly,

(Dheeraj Bhargava)

Enclosure (1)

Specimen-2: Mr. K. Vyasa Rao settles the Telephone Bill.

3762, 32nd Main, 5th Cross,
2nd Stage, Rajajinagar,
BANGALORE: 560 010.

08/06/2006

The Customer Service Centre (Vijayanagar),
Vikram Complex,
Opp to: Navrang Park,
Rajajinagar, BANGALORE-560010

Dear Sir,

Sub: Payment of Telephone Bill.

I enclose cheque no: 4879651 of date on Syndicate Bank, Yeshwantpur Branch, Bangalore drawn in favour of "RBI A/C AOTD, Bangalore" for Rs. 1,489/- in full settlement of Telephone bill no: 1054160. I also enclose the bill, the main portion of which may please be returned to me for my records after stamping your acknowledgment on it.

Thanking you,

Yours truly,

(Sd)

(K.Vyasa Rao).

Provident Fund

Created by the Government of India under the Provident Fund Act for the benefit of the families of the employed class, Provident Fund intends to support the employees and their families financially during their twilight years. 12% of the employee's salary is deducted every month and paid into his/her Provident Fund account. But what is more important is that the employer is also required to make a matching contribution. However, the employer's contribution of 12% of the salary is credited partly (8.33% of the salary) to the Pension Fund account of the employee and partly (3.67% of the salary) to the Provident Fund account of the employee. Thus, effectively, 15.67%(12+3.67) of the employee's salary goes into his/her Provident Fund account and 8.33% the employee's salary goes into his/her Pension Fund account, although the employee contributes only 12% of his/her salary. Interest @ 12% p.a. is calculated at monthly interests and added to the Provident Fund account of the employee. As and when the employee retires, he/she will have some resource to fall back upon, viz., the accumulated balance in his/her Provident Fund account and the monthly pension that he/she will receive from the Pension Fund account.

The employer submits a statement every month to the PF office, after paying into the bank the employee's as well as the employer's contribution for credit of the Provident Fund account and Pension Fund account of the employee, as explained above.

Specimen-1: ABC Ltd., submits the monthly returns to the Office of the Provident Fund Commissioner.

ABC LIMITED
"El Dorado"
#521, F.M. Road, Fort, MUMBAI: 400 001.

Tel: 022-2354 5648
SBI/PF/312

July 15, 2006

The Regional Provident Fund Commissioner,
MUMBAI: 400 001.

Dear Sir,

Sub: Provident Fund and Pension Fund remittance for June, 2006.

We enclose:

1. Challan supporting the remittance of Provident Fund and Pension Fund of our staff into the State Bank of India.
2. Details of Provident Fund deducted from the various employees and the company's contribution thereto in the prescribed form.

Thanking you,

Yours truly,
For ABC LIMITED,
(Goutham Aradhya),
Authorised Signatory

Sales Tax

Sales Tax is in the concurrent list, which means that it is a Central as well as State legislation. Sales tax is intended to help the States raise resources for their development. As the very name suggests, sales tax arises whenever sale of a movable property takes place. Sales tax is levied in various slabs like 2%, 3%, etc., in accordance with the provisions of the Sales Tax Act for the time being in force in a given State. Sales tax rates may be hiked or cut or exempted in respect of any goods, in accordance with the budget proposals passed by the State Legislature concerned.

Registration under the Sales Tax Act is mandatory once the turnover of a dealer exceeds the limit prescribed under the Act. Presently it is Rs. 2,00,000 in Karnataka. Sales tax is collected at the prescribed rate and passed on to the government by the dealer as laid down in the Rules framed under the Act. The dealer includes sales tax in the price of the goods sold to the customer. In other words, the customer pays sales tax to the government through the dealer. Hence, Sales tax is called an indirect tax. Other examples of indirect tax are Central Excise, Customs, etc. The rules require that the dealer file a return every month in the prescribed form (In Karnataka it is called Form: 3), enclosing, thereto the payment towards sales tax for the month. Central Sales Tax comes into the picture only when there is inter-State movement of goods subsequent to sale. In these cases, it overrides the State Sales Tax.

Specimen-1: Gowda & Gowda write to the Commercial Tax Officer enclosing a cheque representing the sales tax payable for the month of June, 2006.

GOWDA & GOWDA,
312, Mission Road,
BANGALORE: 560 027.

June 8, 2006.

The Commercial Tax Officer,
34th Circle,
BANGALORE: 560 001.

Dear Sir,

Sub: Payment of Sales Tax for May 2006.

Enclosed is Form-3 for May 2006 together with a cheque for Rs. 9,281/- on Vijaya Bank, Trinity Circle Branch, Bangalore, drawn in your favour, representing the sales tax payable for the month of June,

Thanking you,

Yours truly,
(R. Ninge Gowda)
Authorised Signatory.

IncomeTax Deducted at Source (TDS)

Income tax is the most important direct tax that the Government of India levies. The Government of India prescribes every year, the rates of taxes and the threshold limits in respect of different categories of taxpayers in accordance with their status. For example, in the case of an individual under the provisions of the Income Tax Act, once the taxable income crosses the threshold limit, a Return is to be filed even if no tax was due to the Government of India. For the financial year 1998-99, this threshold limit is Rs. 50,000. But, in practice, people refrain from filing the Return if no tax is due to the Government of India under the Act. Knowingly or unknowingly such people manage to stay out of the Income tax net. This precisely is one of the reasons that prompted the Government of India to enforce deduction of income tax at source. Accordingly, tax is to be deducted at the prescribed rate by the person making payment of certain incomes and paid to the Government of India through designated banks.

For example, when salary is paid to an employee, the employer is liable to deduct the applicable income tax and pay only the net amount to the employee. The tax so deducted should be paid to the Government of India. The payee will be issued a Tax Deduction Certificate under the Act, in lieu of the deduction effected from his/her payment. The employee will use this Certificate to adjust against the tax payable by him/her while filing his/her Return.

Tax is also deducted at source when a person pays income in the nature of interest or pays to contractors for carrying out any work or pays professional charges or pays technical know-how fee, etc. The payee can claim refund, if any, of the tax so deducted at source only by filing his/her own Return under the Act. Thus, the payee is constrained to return his/her income, thereby adding to the list of Income tax assesses in the country. At the end of the financial year, the employer has to submit a statement in the prescribed form to the Income Tax office concerned, enclosing thereto the copies of the challans supporting the payment to the Government of India of the tax deducted at source and copies of the TDS certificates issued.

STUDY QUESTIONS

Section A

(2 marks Questions - Answer in 4 lines each)

1. What do you understand by Overdraft?
2. Give the meaning of cash credit.

3. What is Letter of Credit?

4. What is a circular letter of credit?

Section B

(8 and 15 marks questions)

1. Write a letter as from the manager of National Bank to one of its customers, informing him that his facility to overdraw his account as being withdrawn since he has not used it for over nine months.

2. A stationery dealer has asked his banker for an overdraft facility of Rs. 15,000 for six months, without security. His business is a reputed one, Draft the reply of the banker (both positive and negative separately).

3. Dhanalakshmi Bank has sanctioned a loan of Rs. 50,000 against the security of company shares valued then at Rs. 80,000. Now the value of these shares has come down by 25%. Write to the customer informing him to give more security to cover the gap caused by fall in value.

4. The deposit of customer has matured and now, he seeks the advice of the bank concerning safe investment with steady income. Draft the bank's reply.

5. A customer would like to raise a loan of Rs. 10,000 against the security of insurance policy. Draft a reply from the banker stating that the loan of fifty percent of the surrender value of the policy can be considered as the policy is in force.

6. A self-employed person has approached a banker for a loan of Rs.40,000 to purchase a xerox machine. Draft a letter as written from the bank explaining how the bank can assist him.

7. As the Secretary of a public limited company, apply to your banker for a medium term loan of Rs. 10 lakhs.

8. As a customer of your bank, draft a letter requesting them for a bill-discounting facility upto Rs.2 lakhs and cheque discounting facility upto Rs. one lakh.

9. Draft a suitable reply from the banker for the problem 8.

10. You have an account with Karnataka Bank, Srirampuram Branch, Bangalore. You are now transferred to Tiptur. Write a suitable letter to the Manager of Bangalore branch to transfer the account to Tiptur Branch. Also forward a copy to the Manager of Tiptur Branch.

11. A trader wants to open a current account with National Bank Ltd. Draft a suitable letter requesting the bank to open the account.

12. A Bank has received a letter enquiring the credit standing of one of your customers. Draft a favourable reply from the bank.

13. Write a letter as from the manager of a bank to an irregular customer asking to close his account whose cheques are frequently bouncing for want of funds at his credit.

14. A village branch of a bank is working at loss, the Board of Management is contemplating to close it. However, they have sought the opinion of the branch manager. Draft a letter as the manager of that branch proposing some change to improve the condition and not to close the branch.

15. Bright Marketers (P) Ltd., Bangalore, who are the markerters of Pharmaceutical products, now operating only in Karnataka would like to expand their marketing operations in Tamil Nadu and Kerala states. They are deputing their marketing manager to explore the market conditions in these states. They have approached you to issue a circular letter of credit to their marketing manager Mr. Raghunandan for a sum of Rs. 50,000 to be used if need be, on his tour. Draft a suitable letter of credit.

16. Write a letter to your banker to confirm a telegram stopping payment of one of your cheques, issued five days ago.

17. A letter has been sent to a valued customer whose account is in credit, stating that his account has been overdrawn. Draft a letter from the banker to the customer apologising for the mistake committed.

18. As a secretary of a public limited company write a suitable letter to your banker requesting him for a guarantee limit upto Rs.25 lakhs.

19. A customer of a bank is complaining that his current account has been heavily debited for Bank charges. Draft a letter as banker, giving reasons for such heavy charges debited to the account.

20. As the manager of a bank in Bangalore write to ANZ Grindlays Bank, London for opening letters of credit with them.

Additional Questions

Part - A (2 to 3 marks)

1. What do you mean by Insurance claim?

2. What is Life Insurance?

3. What is Provident Fund?

4. What is TDS?

5. What is Sales Tax?

Part - B & C

(8 and 15 marks)

1. Write a letter to LIC, local branch to settle your claim on the policy which is matured.
2. Write a letter to P.F. Commissioner requesting him to sanctior loan on your P.F. account.
3. Draft a letter to P.F. Commissioner requesting him to intimate the balance of P.F. in your account including management contribution.
4. Draft a letter to manager, Telecom of your district to give the details regarding new telephone connection.
5. Draft a letter to Commercial Tax Officer requesting him to send your assessment order for the payment of balance tax.

*****

CHAPTER 4

PURCHASE CORRESPONDENCE

- Trade Enquiries and Replies
- Enquiries
- Replies

Request for quotations, tenders, samples and drawings, complaints and follow up.

TRADE ENQUIRIES AND REPLIES

"Trade denotes buy and sell and connotes a commercial course". This has an implication of transaction. The function of trade is to transfer ownership. 'Trade' helps in 2 ways: (a) famine and excessive prices are avoided and (b) diminution in value and waste are largely presented. 'Trade' is therefore a perennial phenomenon in the progressive human society. An individual in the field of trade involving goods and services will have to either be a supplier or a customer. Since both these conduct their trade not in proximity to each other but, in different places, exchange of written thoughts is quite essential between them. When it relates to the ascertainment of availability of specific goods, it is called "Trade Enquiry". For the purchaser the points to consider are (a) The finding of good sources of supply (b) a careful selection of suitable goods as regards both variety and quality and (c) the utilisation of the cheapest means of transport in order to procure the goods on the most advantages terms. The points for the seller are (a) The choice of a good business site (b) the employment of suitable staff (c) the attraction of sufficient customers (d) a pleasing exhibition of goods offered for sale (e) careful treatment of customers (f) orderliness in every direction and (g) suitable methods of advertising.

Business Letters and Their Classifications:

Business situation is never a static factor. In a series of socio–economic conditions characterised by perpetual dynamism associated with disproportionate degrees of change in gifts of nature to human kingdom, both supply of and demand for goods remain a variable factor As a corollary, initiation, presentation, transmission, admission, assimilation, execution, application, documentation, re–transmission, justification, examination, submission, cancellation, recommendation, investigation, quotation, circulation, attestation, confirmation, intimation, incorporation, clarification, pacification, collection, termination so on and so forth, will be seen between buyer and seller.

Hence, it is not an easy task to create divergent business–letters. Classification may be at the most a matter of convenience but not an exhaustive one. Anyhow, for providing a possible coverage, following list may be considered:

1. Enquiry and Reply.
2. Offers and Quotation.
3. Orders – Execution and Cancellation.
4. Claims, Complaints and Settlement of Accounts.
5. Circular Letters.
6. Agency Letters.

7. Status Enquiries.
8. Collection Letter.
9. Application for a situation.
10. Letters of Recommendation and Letters of credit.
11. Bank Correspondence.
12. Letters relating to Export and Import.
13. Insurance Correspondence.
14. Letters to Editors.
15. Correspondence with Government and Public Bodies.
16. Correspondence of a Company Secretary.

Different Letters will depend upon the nature of circumstances. Certain firms have their letters in print in a standard form. It saves time and need for writing letters every now and then. But, personal element is not found in such a letter–writing. If the exact use does not suit the situation, certain modification may be effected.

ENQUIRIES

Enquiries may be (a) Solicited or (b) Unsolicited or (c) for some favour or a routine enquiry

(a) ***Solicited Enquiry:*** means the buyer makes an enquiry quoting the advertisement given by the seller of publicity made by the seller.

(b) ***Unsolicited Enquiry:*** means the buyer makes an enquiry at his own instance or initiation for the first time.

(c) ***Enquiry for some favour:*** means the buyer may not have intention to purchase goods but may be in need of some information like special price or favourable terms offered by the seller.

(d) ***Routine Enquiry:*** means the old customers may write letters to enquire about some usual information.

An enquiry letter may be as short as one line requesting for a price list or a catalogue or sample desired by the buyer which the seller may send. A bit prolonged letter of enquiry may contain classification regarding terms of sale or special price.

Nature of an Enquiry Letter (Features)

(a) Direct, concise and not harsh in expression

(b) Self confidence and optimistic attitude in intentions

(c) Short and pointed, still unambiguous, full and perfect.

How to write an Enquiry Letter – some necessary points and procedure:

(1) Mention the object of enquiry – is it merchandise, classification of service –details or any other bit of information wanted?

(2) Make an appeal for sending the price list catalogue, etc.

(3) Express your desire for getting samples or for showing the actual working of the system in your presence.

(4) Is it personal source or any publication in the paper or magazine you learnt from.

(5) Give your business information and interests.

(6) Demand for the details pertaining to allowance of discount, granting or credit, method of transporting and delivery goods, packing method and charges thereof and payment of such expenses–order–placement will be facilitated much by seeking more details.

(7) An idea of the probable size of the order need be given.

(8) Mention of Budgeted sales volume, confidence in pushing up the sales, financial ability, etc., will enable the seller to grant some concession in price or to decide upon granting sole selling agency in the area along with huge and regular orders will help the seller to make an appropriate decision in the matter.

In a nutshell, in any enquiry letter, one must consider the points like (a) A detailed description of desirable goods, (b) price, time and place of delivery i.e., FOB, FOR, CIF. Ex– Warehouse, Quality as found in sample (c) Terms of payment i.e., C.O.D., C.W.O. on credit, Buyer's financial position, probable purchase size etc. and (d) Other charges like, Insurance, commission, discount, rebate, packing, forwarding, shortest route to the destination etc.

Examples of Opening Sentences

1. Will you kindly quote us the lowest prices for....
2. We desire your samples to be sent to us soon, only then we shall place....
3. Kindly mail us your updated catalogue and price list of....
4. May we demand of you to sent to us your current terms and condition
5. Your name has been suggested to us by M/s....
6. We shall be happy to get detailed information regarding your....

Examples of Closing Sentences

1. Will you kindly write your response at an early date....
2. In case your terms are up to our satisfaction, we shall place our order with you....
3. Kindly consider our enquiry as urgent.
4. On hearing from you , we shall place a firm order with your.
5. We look forward to placing an order with you, if your quotation is suitable to us.
6. As we want to replenish our stock, please let us have your reply within a week.

REPLIES

All the letters of enquiry should be answered in time. If the seller has no stock of the goods asked for by the purchaser, a word of reply is desirable. It implies business, etiquette, respect and interest on the part of the seller.

Routine response should include prices, quotations, discount, credit, delivery and a word of courtesy like " thank you for your interest to deal with us", etc.. A reference to the price–list and quotations as may be enclosed in the letter, if needed.

Response to present a loyal customer should always be in full with dependable information, accurate and correct manner. A word of politeness and thankfulness should be mentioned in such letters invariably.

Response to potential or first time correspondents or customers should be a bit away from the routine style. Our response should turn them into buyers. It must have sales promotion orientation either of the present market product or a new product being invented and to be introduced. Some tactics of salesmen should find a wordy expression in our letter to fetch it a ready market. Arousing interest, buying decisive creation and a forceful explanation to convince him of the nature of product. All·this is a must.

Hints on drafting a reply:

(1) Courtesy, and appreciation.

(2) Reference Date and Number.

(3) Cheerful tone.

(4) A brief note on goods, price reduction, terms and conditions to his advantage.

(5) Order execution period, where and how to deliver goods. Method of payment trade and cash discount, packing of goods and type desired.

(6) How long the offer is kept open.

(7) Details of enclosures like price–list, catalogue, etc.

(8) Show wordy expression of salesman to arouse interest in the customer.

(9) Express your remains to provide any more information which may be required.

An enquiry even when suitably replied, may not result in an order at once. A businessman makes a comparison with all other terms offered to him. He may be forced to bargain to secure more favourable terms i.e., for price– reduction, for better quality at the same price or for a higher discount, etc,. A trader must carefully follow the trend of the market reports, news papers, price lists and salesman's reports. Normally, a trader does not change his source of supply. He should stock the goods on the most advantages terms. He is free to alter his source of supply.

Quotation:

In its Latin Origin 'quotus', it means 'of what number and also 'quot' which means 'how many' . "Quotation" also means 'to give the current price of or 'price quoted'. The terms, 'offers and quotations' are often used synonymously, 'offer' means 'to hold out for acceptance or rejection' or 'propose to give or sell' offering may serve two purposes like, (a) business expansion and (b) service to a large number of customers. There is a slight difference between an 'offer' and a 'quotation'. Offer is made to a large number of customers; it may be written in general terms and it takes the form of a printed. But, when the offer is specific, it is applicable only to the specified article and is sent to the enquirer only.

Since the quotation is supplied in reply into an enquiry, the specific offer is synonymous to the quotation. An offer opens up new markets. It may make the dormant market quite brisk. An offer should simply give our facts regarding increased demand, small stock etc,. The chief points in making an offer are : (a) Nature of goods (quality) (b) The measure or weight (unit) (c) The currency of payment (d) The terms of payment–cash or credit (e) The mode and place of delivery (whether ex–warehouse, f.o.b or franco, etc,) and also whether by post, courier, train, lighter, steamer sailing vessel or tug. (f) The firm of delivery considering possible delay to be manufactured to order or obtain elsewhere, fine imposed for exceeding the time stipluated etc.

'Firm offer' means an order will be accepted at the specified price and conditions, within the specified time only.

'Offer without engagement' means order at the specified price may not be accepted without negotiation.

Finally we may say that an Enquiry implies some interest in goods – therefore, replies to enquiries should be made without any excuse for delay. It is an opportunity to promote sales. It provides the chance of establishing a long trade connection. A favourable impression of the firm should be created (a) Reply should not be vague. (b) It is to be an effective sales letter (c) Lifeless reply does not impress the enquiries (d) It should not lack in its appeal.

Terms used in Offers and Quotations:

(1) ***At station:*** Seller's cost upto Railway Station and afterwards, buyer pays carriage cost.

(2) ***Ex. works/Warehouse:*** It represents price of goods at seller's warehouse and buyer pays for conveyance from seller's warehouse point.

(3) ***Free on Rail (F.O.R):*** Here price includes all charges.

(4) *Carriage Paid:* Seller will pay transport charges.

(5) *Carriage Forward (Carr. fwd):* It is practically F.O. R. Here buyer will bear the carriage and transport charges.

(6) *Cash on delivery (C.O.D.):* Buyer will pay on delivery of goods to him.

(7) *Cash with Order (C.W.O.):* Order will be executed only when payment is made along with the order.

(8) *Prompt cash:* Payment on Delivery of goods, only 2 or 3 days will be allowed for examining the goods.

(9) *Net/Nett:*

(a) Original amount – deductions = Amount to be paid finally

(b) Gross Weight = Case/Wrapers Weight =Actual weight of goods (Net)

(10) *3 percent, 7days:* From the date of Invoice if the payment is made within 7days, 3% will be allowed.

(11) *Loco:* Price at seller's warehouse/factory and buyer will meet all conveyance cost to buyers place but here 'price' at warehouse of seller may or may not include cost of packing. It should be specified in the quotation whether cost of packing is extra or not.

(12) *Indent:* An order for purchase of goods with full particulars.

(13) *Price current:* A list of market prices of goods.

(14) *Prompt:* The credit of time allowed for the payment of parcel goods.

(15) *Tare:* A deduction from the goods weight allowed for the weight of the cask, bag, chest, etc.,

(16) *Tret:* An allowance of 4 lb, on every 104 lb on certain articles of merchandise for dust.

(17) *E.&O.E.:* (Errors and omissions Expected) usually printed at the bottom left hand corner of an invoice, according to which the seller has the right of making corrections of errors or ommissions, if any.

(18) *Forwarding note:* A note prepared in a prescribed form by the consignor of goods by railway giving the particulars of goods consigned and the name and address of the consignee.

Let us consider the examples of Enquiries, Replies and Quotations in the following pages for a thorough grasp of it.

Example 1:

Enquiry for Timber

215, Coconut Street,
K.R. Extension, Tiptur.
13th October, 2006

The Timber Supply Association
268, Uphill Street,
Sakaleshpur.

Dear Sir,

Please let me know your latest price and the earliest date of delivery for a lot of 500 Burma Teak logs, prime quality, plain straight grown free from worm and shakes, two to three feet thick, some logs to be at least twenty to twenty five feet long.

Payment, measurement and all other conditions as formerly agreed.

Yours faithfully,
Sadashiva

Example 2: Asking for price list

VIGHNESWARA FURNITURE COMPANY

216, Hill Estate
Bijavara – 2
16th December, 2006

Harihareshwara Furniture Company
62, Temple Street,
Madhugiri – 6.

Dear Sirs,

Please send us your latest illustrated price list and also inform us of your best terms for bulk purchase.

Yours faithfully
Vigneshwara Furniture Company

Example 3: Reply to letter in Example 1

HARIHARESHWARA FURNITURE COMPANY

62, Temple Street
Madhugiri
19th December, 2006

VIGNESHWARA FURNITURE COMPANY
216, Hill Estate
Bijavara – 1.

Dear Sir,

We thank you for your enquiry of 16th Dec. 2006, and we have pleasure in sending you a copy of our illustrated price list enclosed in this letter.

Our 'Vigneshwar Idol' symbol has rich experience of six decades backing its quality in creating quality articles of furniture for modern needs.

Our normal Trade discount is 15% and 8% extra only for bulk orders exceeding Rs. 20,000/–

It will be our pleasure to meet your needs.

Yours Faithfully,
For Harihareshwara Furniture Co.,
S. Rao (Sales Manager).

Example 4:

INQUIRY FORM

Phone : 2482424 (31ines)

BHIMAKAYA LIMITED

Rose field House, Farm Road, Tavaka Estate,
P.O. Box No. 832, Bangalore – 4.
No. PEZ/468
Date : 23rd January 2006

To,
VAJRA SHRESTA COMPANY PRIVATE LTD.,
9, Tank Street,
Tumkur – 8.

Please quote your lowest price by return of post for the under quoted.

FOR VAJRASHRESTA COMPANY LTD.,

DELIVERY TIME TO BE STATED _____

Indent No.	Code No.	Description	Qty	Unit	Rate Rs. P.	Delivery
1.		1% Carbon Steel 1.3/8" Sq.	6 Cwts			
2.		1% Carbon Steel 1.5/8" Sq.	35 Cwts			
		Specification Carbon : 1% Manganese not more than 30% Varadium : 25%				

Example 5: Request for Catalogue

PRAJWALYA MANA

Electrical Accessory Dealer

Telephone : 52368
Telegraph : "Light Button"

35, Tank Bund Road,
J.M. Extension,
Bangalore – 16,
21st August 2006

The Deepa Electrical Supply Co. Ltd.,
16/A, Vanatheyan Street,
N.R. Colony, Kolar – 5.

Dear Sir,

Will you kindly send me a copy of your whole sale catalogue?

There is a large demand locally for your class orders of an average value of Rs.80,000. In this circumstances, please inform me what are the best discounts you can grant me from list prices and so enable me to consider promptly what the prospects are of doing business with you.

Yours faithfully,
Prajwalyamana

Example 6: Enclosing Catalogue of Electrical Appliances (Reply to letter of Example No.4)

THE DEEPA ELECTRICAL SUPPLY CO., LTD.,

16/A, Vainatheyan Street,
N.R. Colony, Kolar–5
23rd August, 2006

Mr. Prajwalyamana
355, Tank Bund Road,
J.M. Extension, Bangalore– 16

Dear Sir,

We have received your letter of 21st August, '98 and are sending you by post our wholesale catalogue of electrical appliances.

We have stated our lowest prices as well as our conditions of sale. We allow 3.5% discount for cash within one month from the date of invoice and a further 4.5% for orders of Rs.25,000 or more. Carriage will be borne by us in Kolar.

Our competitors can offer you no better terms than these and therefore, we look forward to the pleasure of recording our first transaction with you in the near future.

As per our trade customers, when you place your first order with us, please name two trade references. It will help us to handle your order expeditiously.

Yours faithfully,
The Deepa Electrical Supply Co. Ltd.
Varabhanu,
Manager.

Example 7: Quotation for Teak Logs

(Reply to letter of Example No. 1)

THE TIMBER SUPPLY ASSOCIATION

268, Uphill Street,
Sakaleshpur.
18th Oct. 2006

Sri Saindhava
215, Coconut Street,
K.R. Extension, Tiptur.

Dear Sir,

We thank you for your enquiry of 13th Oct. 2006. We are able to supply you with 500 logs Burma Teak, Prime quality, plain straight grown, free from worm or shakes, 2–3 ft. thick, some logs to be 20–25 ft. long, at the price of Rs.80.00 per foot, c.i.f. Tiptur. We could give you delivery towards the end of next month.

If you place an order with us, you may be certain of our active co–operation in your selection.

Yours faithfully,
Per pro. The Timber Supply Association,
P. Varyadhipa (Manager).

Example 8: Inquiry Regarding Machinery

134, Mela Street,
Behind Bus Stand,
B.P. Road, Sira.
3rd May 2006.

Sri. Chamtkara Bharita Yantra Karyagara,
116/B, Old Chennai Road,
Bangalore – 17.

Dear Sir,

We got your address from Sri. Vilasa Vantha. Now, we are sending you the enclosed drawings of three pumping machines.

Will you kindly let us know the price at which you could supply them and the delivery date. We want them before the end of July 2006.

We shall have to buy some more equipment to have our complete We shall place further orders if the initial machines are upto mark.

Yours faithfully,
Yanthrik Balayuth.

Example 9: Submitting Quotation
(Reply to letter of Example No.8)

Yanthrakaryagara
116/B, Old Chennai Road
Bangalore – 17.
8th May, 2006

Messrs. Yathrik and Balayuth
134, Mela Street,
Behind Bus Stand,
SIRA.

Dear Sir,

Your letter dated 3rd May, 2006 has been on my table informing us of your need for 3 pump sets. I hope that I will supply your needs. I also hope that you are thinking of placing your order for those with me soon.

I shall supply 3 machines as per design and drawings sent to me. My pricing is as follows:

(1)	Machine – Core Design – 89	Model No. F.I3	Rs. 44,750.00
(2)	Machine – 'Sputime' – 90	Model No. X.27	Rs. 56,230.00

(3) Machine – "Fly"–91 Model No.BJ–8 Rs.62,350.00

Ex–works Bangalore –17, net cash against 3 months acceptance. Delivery will be made by the end of July, 98.

Lowest possible prices are specially quoted for you and I hope to receive your order. Since the time span is too short, perhaps, you send your order in written communication to me.

Yours faithfully,

Chitanya

Tenders

A tender is quite simply a statement of the price at which one offers to carry out work, supply goods or services, etc. For example, the Public Works Department may invite tenders for a new bridge or the Highways Department may invite tenders for the construction of a new motorway.

Specimen 1: The following is a tender invited by the CPRI, Bangalore for the construction of CSET in CPRI campus.

CENTRAL POWER RESEARCH INSTITUTE

Prof. Sir C.V. Raman Road, Sadashivnagar Sub-Post Office,
Post Box No: 8066, Bangalore.– 560 080.

Civil Engineering Division

Sealed item rate tenders in the prescribed form are invited from Registered Contractors in State PWD, CPWD, Railways, MES who have done similar works for the execution:

Sl. No.	Name of the work	Estimated cost put to Tender (Rs. in La)	Time for comple	Earnest Money Deposit Rs	Class of Contractor	Cost of Tender Docum Rs.
1.	Constru CSET in CRPI campus	36.00	8 months	90,000/–	1 and above	500.00

Tender documents will be issued to those tenderers who can satisfy CPRI on the basis of their past performance, experience in execution of similar type of work, their financial capability, technical manpower, etc. Separate request for issue of tender application forms should accompany the details as required above. They are required to produce certificates regarding latest Income Tax Clearance Certificate, Works Experience Certificates at the time of request for tender documents. Application for tender documents would be received **from 03.08.2006 and 04.08.2006 and blank tender documents would be issued from 07.08.2006 & 10.08.2006** from the office of the undersigned on payment of cost towards documents in cash.

The tenderers must submit sealed tenders with the name of the work superscribed on the cover duly completed in all respects to the undersigned on or **before 3.00 p.m. on 14.08.2006 and the tenders** will be opened at 3.30 p.m. on the same day in the presence of the tenderers or their authorised representatives who are present at that time. Tender should be accompanied by the EMD in the form of Demand Draft drawn in favour of **Accounts Officer, CPRI, Bangalore.** The undersigned reserves the right to accept or reject any or all tenders without assigning any reason thereof.

Sd/– Head CED

Example 10: Confirmation of Telegraphic Enquiry

41, Maiden Road
School Zone, R.T. Nagar
Bangalore – 4.
3rd Sept. 2006

Mr. Thomson
Marvel Cotton Warehouse
444, Hubli Road,
Davangere–2.

Dear Sir,

I confirm my telegram of this morning as follows :

"Please quote lowest 100 bales' good Texas' delivery October.

I await receipt of your lowest price and terms.

Yours Faithfully,
James Ruthell.

Example 11: (Reply to letter of Example No.9)

Marvel Cotton Warehouse
444, Hubli Road
Davangere–2
9th Sept. 206

Mr. James Ruthell,
41, Maiden Road,
R.T. Nagar, Bangalore – 4.

Dear Sir,

We received your letters dated 3rd Sept.2006 and 6th Sept, 2006 and confirming the said telegram.

I can offer you good Texas cotton 100 bales at Rs.16 per kg. deducting the weight of the hoops, and 4% for tare. Delivery in October ex–warehouse here.

The terms of payment would be three months net or 11.4% discount for cash on the total invoices, amount inclusive of all expenses.

We are awaiting your instructions.

Yours faithfully,

Example 12: Enquiry for Printing

NAVA GRANTHA COMPANY, PRIVATE LTD.,

Pustaka Mahal,
124, Delhi Road, D.T. Street,
Malleshwaram, Bangalore – 3.

14th January, 2006.

The Chaitanya Printing Works Ltd.
39, Vedavyasa Street, Shakar Mutt Extension,
BANGALORE – 18.

Dear Sir,

We are forwarding the manuscript of our publication. "Business Letters Styles" with the bearer and shall be pleased to get from you, your lowest quotations for printing 4000 copies of the same. 40 lb. D/Crown glazed Indian paper, binding them in twinkling cloth and wrapping them in jackets of 72 lb coloured art paper–

Please favour with your early reply.

Yours faithfully,
Nava Grantha Company Pvt. Ltd.
R.G. Naipunya,
Director.

Example 13: Quotation for Printing

Estimate No.4456

THE CHAITANYA PRINTING WORKS LTD.

39, Vedavyasa Street,

Shankarmutt Extension Bangalore – 18.

4th April 2006

The Novelty Book Company Private Ltd.

122, Maruthi Road,

Vijayapura Extension,

Bangalore – 70.

Dear Sir,

We thank you for your enquiry dated 26th March, 2006. We have pleasure in providing you with our quotation as under:

Details	**Qty**	**Price Rs. P.**	**Remarks**
For Printing and supplying "Business Letters–Styles" D/Crown 1/6 Size set in 10 or 12 pt. and printed in Black on 40 lb. D/Crown glazed paper as under :			
Text Matter (with paper)	1000 copies	300.00	per page
Text Matter (without paper)	1000 copies	100.00	per page
Wrapper Printing in single colour on 72 lb.D /	1000 copies	3,300.00	lot
Crown Art or Buff paper – do – (without paper)	– do –	900.00	– do –
Binding full cloth (Samples of paper enclosed)	– do –	3,500.00	– do –

We fervently hope that our prices are satisfactory and you will send your order at an early date.

Subject to terms printed on the reverse.

Yours faithfully,

For Chaitany Printing Works Ltd.

S. Chatura (Manager).

Example 14: Asking for more favourable terms

MUKESH STORES

142, Cottonpet, Tumkur,
18th Nov. 2006

MESSRS. SETHU RAM & CO.
184, Chowltry Street,
M.K.G. 6th Main, R.V. Extension, Bangalore – 6.

Dear Sirs,

Thank you for your letter dated 14th Nov. 2006 with your design leaflet.

We have also received price lists and their patterns from other firms all over Karnataka, Andhra Pradesh and Chennai also. Their terms appear more attractive. A firm from Ananthapuram and an other from Chennai offer Trade discount of 6% and are ready to despatch the goods carriage paid. We wish to place order for our requirements with you on the condition that at least the very same % of discount is allowed to us.

To enable you to know our financial strength, we refer you to :

1. M/s. Murthy and Co.,
   Woolen Merchants, 74, Empress street,
   Vishwa Nagar, Bangalore – 46.
2. The United Commercial Bank of India,
   B.V.K. Iyengar Road, Bangalore.

Since we are willing to purchase our terrycot, terryne and woollen suitings as early as possible, we are anxious to hear from you soon.

Yours faithfully,
For Mukesh Stores,
M. Vastra.

Example 15: Letter making a firm offer

MANDYA SUGAR COMPANY LIMITED

181, Vilasa Road,
City Market Square,
Bangalore – 4.
January 16th, 2006

GOVARDHAN AND BROTHERS
(Wholesale dealers)
169, Mahashi Road,
Udaya School Extension, TUMKUR.

Dear Sir,

We are glad to write to you that just now, a huge quantity of sugar specially processed in refinement plant to obtain excellent standard is received. Our retail selling price is Rs.6.75 per kg or less than a bag of 100 kgs and for purchase exceeding a quintal, ex–warehouse rate is Rs.6,000/– per bag and 2.5% discount against cash payment in a fortnight period.

Present demand from merchants situated locally may take away 80% of the available stock of sugar. But our 'firm order' to you is upto 10 quintals. We will keep this offer valid upto 4 p.m. on Monday, 30th Jan. 2006.

We believe in your desire to avail this occasional chance.

Yours faithfully,
Per pro Mandya Sugar Co. Ltd.,
Sharkasa Abhilasa,
Sales Manager.

Example: 16 Letter refusing to pay expense

SHOBHAYAMANA PAINTS LIMITED

Lalapet Road,
Madhugiri,
10th May 2006

The Executive Director
Perfect Builders Ltd.,
Devata Mansions,
142, Vivekananda Marg, Abhiyanthara Colony,
Bangalore – 41.

Dear Sir,

Thank you very much for your order of 2nd May 2006 for the 200 kgs of 'sticky shine' and 75 kgs of 'golden shine distemper'. But, we regret to inform you that we are not in a position to send the package by our lorry transport as we are not willing to pay for carriage of goods. Our quoted price in itself has been quite concessional. Moreover, our percentage of profit also is very small.

In the circumstances sincerely detailed here in this letter, we hope that you will alter your conditions and give us a word of your decision to execute the order.

Thank you,

Yours faithfully,
For Shobhayamana Paints Ltd.,
(Gambheeraiah),
Sales Manager.

Complaints – Letters of Complaint

Background: Even if the business is well managed, even if arrangements are previously made and even if terms and conditions are settled, mistakes, misunderstandings, imperfections, deficiencies, creep in. Sometimes differences of opinion may lead to tedious disputes. A reasonable trader may ignore insignificant defects. Of course, to err is common to human being, but, it should not prove a venom to him later. Now let us examine mistakes and errors that would emerge before we consider other aspects of the problem.

Sources of Mistakes and Errors:

1. Incorrect writing of order.
2. Wrong direction to despatch section.
3. Mistake in the invoice preparation in Accounts section.
4. Despatch section's carelessness leading to:
   (a) Wrong quality (b) improper size (c) unasked for brand (d) unwanted pattern (e) undesired quantity (f) improper colour (g) defective measure (weight or scale (h) breakage, evaporation, cut, leakage, pilferage, damage, mutilation, etc., not being seriously examined by irresponsible staff.
5. Defective packing resulting in damage to goods in transit.
6. Article itself might have inherent manufacturing defect.
7. Abnormal delay in sending the consignment.
8. Careless reading of item–wise details in the order.
9. Inferior quality and
10. Disagreement in payment of carriage expenses.

It is not easy to enumeratre the occasions that give rise to letters of complaint. The above noted list is only indicative and those which are common to all types of business houses.

Meaning of Complaint:

Normally, after the delivery of goods by the seller to the buyer, he checks them up and confirms whether the goods sent tally with the details stated then by him in the order. When both the consignment and details or order are in perfect agreement, the buyer need not acknowledge the receipt of goods. But when the discrepancy is discovered, he must bring it to the notice of the supplier, this exactly gives rise to a "a letter of complaint".

CLAIM – Its meaning:

An acceptable cause is the base of the buyer's writing a complaint letter. In so writing, he establishes the fact of his legal right to seek redressal of his grievances. Bringing it to the notice of the seller by the buyer is nothing but, putting forth the claim or loss or damage. Loss may be in the form of expenses to send back the goods or loss of profit due to non-sale of it or damage done to goods needs rectification or replacement and who should pay for those etc.,

Dissatisfied customer may write a discourteous letter. Such a letter will create only displeasure, anger, altercation and uncultured verbal behaviour reduced to written letter. Badly worded letters are more harmful than a venomous bite of a serpent. Courteously worded complaint letter will automatically persuade the seller to realise his mistake and capture the ethical aspects of seller's future course of action.

Hence, it is to the advantage of both the parties to effect an amicable settlement either by exchanging the goods or by making an allowance. This is preferable by taking the matter to the court of law.

Main features of a well drafted complaint letter:

1. Genuineness:
   a. No false statements
   b. No vagueness
   c. A clear draft
2. Completeness:
   a. Full information
   b. Full idea
   c. Logical flow of idea
   d. Only relevant facts of case
3. Sincerre Solicitation:
   a. Nature of inconvenience – a clear exposition
   b. Concrete suggestions
4. Full reference details, provisions i.e.,
   a. Original order
   b. Reference No.
   c. Goods description
   d. Price list
   e. Invoice No.
   f. Delivery Note
5. No Apology but Advice
6. No accusation
7. No. exaggeration
8. No threat

9. No loss of temper
10. No agitation
11. Have confidence
12. No irritation
13. No indignation
14. No supposition
15. No offensiveness.

Writing a complaint letter demands tact, carefulness and the art of convincing. Satisfactory correction is to be aimed at.

How to write a letter of complaint (or claims) – a few guidelines:

(a) Write a clear and complete statement of matter.

(b) Tone and style should be amicable, persuasive and courteous.

(c) Avoid dishonors and casting aspersions attitude.

(d) Avoid curt, abuse and concoction.

(e) Don't write when anger has encircled you.

(f) Give specific order No., Ref. No. Quotation date, arrival of consignment time.

(g) Explain monetary loss or loss of goodwill.

(h) State the rectification steps.

(i) Arrest the seller's mind by being frank and fair as well as humble and honest reply.

Replies to Letter of Complaint or Letters of Adjustments:

Complaints are a regular feature of business life. Complaints may be different types such as :

(a) Frivolous /trivial

(b) True/exaggerated

(c) Serious / normal

(d) Inherent/created

(e) Genuine/spurious

(f) Goods/services

(g) Writing /packing

(h) Discourteous treatment etc.

There is no shame or disgrace in receiving complaints. Unlike in the past now complaints and criticism are invited. Improvement and enormous profits are attributable to soliciting for complaints. Complaints benefit businessmen to survive competition. Legitimate complaints are beneficial. The purpose of a letter of complaint is to point out the defect or fault or error and to bring about rectification or correction of it. The claim will not become tenable unless it is a prompt and satisfactory complaint. Modern tendency is to use the work "Adjustment" in place of undesirable term "complaint".

Whether it is reality or falsity a customer deserves an explanation from the seller. An immediate acknowledgment for having received a letter of complaint should be given to the buyer stating that his claim is under due consideration.

Adjustments are unavoidable. They are a vital part of every business. The success of business depends on it. Adjustment letters can build good will. They have sales potential. Adjustments may be in the form of replacement of goods, repairs at the cost of seller, discounts allowed because of defective nature of goods, charges to be written of, etc.

Regarding worn-out, damaged, inferior in quality, tastelessness, glamour, fine look or shabby look, design, colour, the view points always differ between the buyer and the seller in intensity of feeling and the extent of veracity. Both of them differ normally.

Seller's arguments to refuse or admit complaint may be based on several reasons such as, (a) defects not noticed at the time of purchase (b) careless handling (c) instruction of manufacturer to use ignored (d) product quality has deteriorated due to rough handling, exposure to heat, sun rays, atmospheric changes etc.

Yet, honest solution should be found out for all these problems mutually between the seller and the buyer. They should have both mutual belief and fair play. Adjustments should not be viewed as waste of time, energy and money. Rather they create a real potential for good will. All adjustments must be handled with care, caution, clarity, courtesy, comprehension, conciseness, civility, courage and consideration. Adjustment letters require the most delicate and skilful handling. Because they have to achieve the double object of satisfying the customer and safeguarding the interests and reputation of the writer.

Hints on Writing Adjustment Letter
or
Hints on Writing Replies to Letters of Complaint

1. Write a prompt reply to the complaint letter. Delay causes annoyance–Write a letter of acknowledgment expressing regret. Assure the customer of investigation and due action. In service matters effective way is to send a telegram.

2. If enquiry is well founded, thank the complainant and apologise for the trouble. Explain the reason or mistake. Assure him of its avoidance in future. Give immediate satisfaction.

3. If it is due to misconcept in customer's mind, tell him about his leisurely attitude, or inability to select or wrong judgement. Educate him about his ignorance in a sympathetic and amicable way. Tell him you are ready to serve him and you are eager to offer your services.

4. If it is complaint, not return reason based, make a frank statement of refusal. Inform him of your rational judgement. As seller accept no blame or admit of no responsibility, never certify customer as being dishonest or unworthy.

5. Ignore if the complainant is found to have made a ridicule or mockery or used slang.

You as the seller, try to be reasonable, justifiable, polite, perfect and parliamentary in your working a letter to give a satisfactory and same reply to his complaint.

Example 1: Letter of complaint regarding shortage in quantity (weight)

NANDAGOPALA & SONS

146, Main Road,
Near M.G. Circle,
Tumkur–2.

16th Dec. 2006

THE RELIANCE BUTTER STALL
22/A, I Floor,
Ananda Complex,
Fort Area,
Holenarsipura.

Dear Sir,

We got the box released from 'BABU Transport Co.' and found 24 bottles of clarified butter on 14th Dec. In fact, we felt very happy about the excellent quality butter.

But, we regret to bring to your notice that we had ordered for 30 bottles weighing 1/2 a kg each. Thus, the shortage in weight is 3 kg.

As the shortage costs us Rs.120/– please send us a credit note or the amount being the value of unsent quantity.

Yours faithfully
Nanda gopal
Proprietor.

Example 2: Reply for the above complaint

THE RELIANCE BUTTER STALL

22/A, I Floor
Ananda Complex
Fort Area,
Holenarsipur.

19th Dec. 2006

NANDAGOPALA & SONS,
146, Main Road,
Near M.G. Circle, Tumkur –2.

Dear Sir,

It is with regret I learn from your letter of 16th Dec. that our butter box fell short of 6 half a kg bottles in its contents.

Kindly excuse the mistake of packing assistant in our business stall. There was heavy rush due to weekly fair in the town. Added to this the strange devotees traffic due to the car festival of the presiding deity of this town, he should have had a lot of tension in mind.

We are extremely sorry that this cause of complaint must have upset you.

We are sending you the credit note for the deficiency costing Rs.120–

We are happy at least quality of butter has pacified your anger to make you write your complaint with calmness.

Yours faithfully,
For Reliance Butter Stall,
G. Bennekrishna,
Manager.

Example 3: Letter of complaint regarding shortage of ordered quantum

BHAT AND COMPANY

89, N. Raju Road,
K.T. Bhashyam Circle,
K.R. Puram, Koratagere,
21st May, 2006.

M/S. AHMED AND CO.,
28/9, Pushpa Road,
Near Sangeetha Palace, Tumkur – 4.

Dear Sir,

Kindly read our order of 12th May, bearing No.268/WS on the basis of your 9th May, price list supplied by you. We placed an order for 1200 kilograms of Bengal Gram. You have sent us 120 packets of 10 kgs each. But 13 packets contain half the wanted quantity. Please ascertain and inform us the reason for it. How will you ask us to adjust is left to you to consider.

We await your response.

Yours faithfully,
for Bhat & Co.,
D.N. Undal.

Example 4: Reply to letter No.3

Date 22nd May, 2006

Dear Sir,

We are very sorry to hear from your letter of 21st May, about 13 packets containing only 5 kgs instead of usual 10 kgs. Bengal Gram now cost Rs. 20 per kg. Thus, we have to adjust as follows:

Total paid to us 1200 x 20 = Rs.24,000

Supplied 120 packets of which 107

packs x 10 kgs = 1070 x 20 = 21,400

Balance 2,600

Less cost of 13 pkts x 5Kg @Rs.20 –1300

Net payable 1300

∴ We will be sending you a cheque in your favour for Rs. 1,300/–. Please excuse us for unintentional deficient packing of your required quantity of Bengal Grams.

Please deem it an unexpected trouble and bear with us to patronise us.

Yours faithfully,
For Ahmed and Co.,
R. Khan (Manager).

Example 5: Letter of complaint for inferior quality

ATTIRE AND WEAR LIMITED

182, Exhibit Mahal
Church Road,
Mysore – 4'

26th Oct. 2006

M/S JOHN STRONG & CO,
46, Annibesent Road,
Daryaganj Extension,
Chennai – 26.

Dear Sir,

Please refer to our order no. TC/86 of 22nd Oct. 2006. We have ordered for 2500 Table Cloth pieces measuring 11/4x2 metre pink colour. But, you have sent all of them in Ash colour. Here customers do not prefer to go in for Ash colour. We have to sell them @5 to 10% discount. Atleast if you allow us 7 1/2 % discount, we can keep this for sale.

Otherwise, please inform us as to how to expect replacement of it from you.

Yours faithfully,

For Attire and Wear Ltd.,

Example 6: Reply to letter No. 5

Dear Sir,

We regret the mistake caused in sending the cloth of colour of your preference. The quality of texture of ash colour is superior to other colours.

In fact, our assistant is well versed in packing up the goods and knows by virtue of experience who are our old customers. Probably he packed up the Ash colour cloth for you specifically to give good quality cloth. We would have asked him for details, but he is on leave for 10 days for his daughter's marriage. His intention, we presume was to give you quality cloth but, for your purpose, we deem it unintentional and ask for return of goods at our cost.

We are unable to give you discount for such a fine texture and fast colour. You debit our A/c for expenses thereof.

Yours sincerely,

for M/s. John Strong & Co.

Example 7: Letter of complaint for goods wrongly sent to Buyer

STANDARD BOOKS SELLERS

620, Clever Street,
Cantonment Complex,
Bangalore–5.

18th June 2006

EXCELLENT PUBLISHING HOUSE,
420, Cap Fixing Road,
Walker's Extension,
Utopian City.

Dear Sir,

As per Order No.428 of 16th June, 2006 we ordered for the following:

		Rs. P.
(a)	Financial Accounting Spicer and Pegler – 4 @ Rs.125/– each	500.00
(b)	English and Commercial Correspondence – Nagavoka – 6 @ Rs.100/– each	600.00
(c)	Management Accounting By J. Batty @ Rs.120/– each	720.00
		1,820.00

We thank you for 'Book parcel' which we received in good condition but, it was surprising to note that the following were found on opening the parcel:

		Rs.
(a)	Psychology – 4 Rs. Jan Read @ Rs.80/– each	320.00
(b)	Indian History by Majumdar –4 @ Rs.100/– each	400.00
(c)	Learn Cooking by Sequara – 8 @ Rs.80/– each	640.00
(d)	Commerce by James Stephenson – 4 @ Rs.115/– each	460.00
		Rs. 1820.00

The whole order is an entirely different one and except for total, nothing we ordered tallies. This has fully annoyed us as to imagine how carelessly you have consigned us the goods – rather scant respect to our need. Why this? What do you want us to do next? Reply by return of the post.

Yours truly,

For Standard Book Stall,

M. Kopistha,

Manager.

Example 8: Reply to the complaint as per above Example No. 7

Dear Sir,

We got your letter of 18th June 2006. We are sincerely sorry to note that the books we sent you by parcel should have been sent to a different place.

It is entirely due to casual leave of regular assistant in packing and sorting section.

Your details of what your order was and 'what you got' helped us a lot to locate your real need. Both Bills bearing No.646 and 647 have same total amounts and probably led him to confusion. Hence this mis–packing.

You please send back the parcel at our cost and we will meanwhile despatch your real requirements. We regret the inconvenience caused to you.

Yours faithfully,
For Standard Book Sellers,
P. Sarihoythu,
Manager.

Sample 9: A Letter of complaint for delay in despatch of goods

JATEENDRA DOMESTIC UTENSILS TRADING COMPANY

44, 'Mahadwar',
Chitra Complex Area,
HASSAN.

May 16, 2006

The Sales Manager
Mandovi Pressure Cooker Mfg. Co. Ltd.
Gajibiji Nagar,
Chickmagalur.

Dear Sir,

We regret to state that though we placed an order for 144 pressure cookers of 'Mandavi' trade style, on 25th May, 2006, there is no response from you uptill now.. You ought to have delivered goods well before 1st May, 2006. There was an understanding on this point. Apart from trouble, one of the customers for whom we wanted it, is being irritated over our inability to firmly tell them anything.

That customer is a big business dealer and our future may be much impaired on this count.

In view of this, please inform us as to when the consignment may be expected from you.

In spite of clear understanding you have ignored the importance of the deal with our customer. On this ground alone, we can impute and impeach you in the law court. Even then as an element of cordiality is mutually known to be present between us, we are constrained to await your sending goods by rail upto to May 26, 2006.

We hope that you will not drive us to the doors of justice to seek it from you through there. This course of action is not a palatable trade-practice.

Yours faithfully,
For Jathendra Domestic Utensils,
Jatheendran,
Partner – Manager.

Example 10: Reply to the complaint as per above Example No. 9

Dear Sir,

Thank you for your letter of May 16, 2006. We regret that we have made you write a letter of complaint, of course, unavoidably. The entire labour of our factory was outside the premises shouting for wage increase. As such, the plant and machinery were untouched for a fortnight period. Moreover, the pressure cooker of Mandovi type you have ordered for is not available in stores even now. In this moment of confusion we should not be able to honour the implicit terms between us or any customer.

Sorry, we are forced to be dicscourteous in making our stand clear. In times of clamour we presume you are our well wisher. Hence, we also presume to compel you to hear us with sympathetic attitude.

If you bear with us for at least three weeks more, not only pressure cooker of your design will be despatched to you but any new orders as well from you and others.

We still expect you to credit us with cordiality which is mutual and unbroken. Please lend your helping hand by being a sympathetic and order placer only with us. Our conscience keeps the doors of justice always open for both of us. Your order and prompt execution of it will remain our trade practice.

Please visit us in person or phone us up to be mutually cordial.

Yours faithfully,
For Jateendra Domestic
Utensils Trading Co.,
Abhaya Pradhan,
Sales Manager.

Follow-up Letters:

These letters are mainly concerned with sales circulars. When any reply is not received for sales letters the firm can try again with a different appeal and an altogether ne approach.

Writing again to catch the mind of customer and make him swing into action is called "Follow–up Letter". A new line of approach should be adopted, emphasising new points of the product. The tone of the follow–up letter should not be offensive. A good follow–up letter converts the prospect into customer and old customers continue to stay with the firm. While drafting a follow–up letter the following points are to be borne in mind.

(i) It should be drafted to satisfy the desire and thinking oi particular class of people for whom the product is designed.

(ii) There should be less time–gap between the first and second letter.

(iii) The follow–up letters should be different from that of the original circular. The contents should not be repetitive.

(iv) It should be positive and should not give room for the customer that the firm is disappointed by less enquiries after the issue of first letter.

(v) Test the message of second letter by sending only few letters. If the customers respond, release them in more number. If the response is negative, change the tone of the letter to suit the needs of the customer.

Following is the specimen follow–up letter concerning a circular issued earlier.

July 15, 2006

Dear Customer,

DHANWANTRI SLIMMER SYSTEM is perfect equipment to reduce body weight. We are happy to note that this system has attracted the customers in the market, ever since it is released.

We are pleased to inform you that we are giving a 5% special discount on sales price for the first 500 customers. Why should you not be one of such customers? Very few pieces are left to fill up the 500 mark. Act quickly and get a handsome discount. Our representative will visit you on request to demonstrate the equipment. Visit us to know more about the equipment. Yours for improved fitness.

For Dhanwantri Slimmer
System,
(Sd) Managing Director.

STUDY QUESTIONS

Section A

(2 Marks Questions - Answer in 4 lines each)

1. What does complaint mean?

2. Mention four sources of mistakes and errors.

3. What do you mean by 'claim' in business letter of complaint?
4. Draw a line of distinction between complaint and claim.
5. Mention four main features of a well drafted complaint letter.
6. Do you support threat, exaggeration, excitement and apology in a complaint letter.
7. Write any four guidelines to draft a good complaint letter.
8. Mention any four types of complaints.
9. Is complaint a shameful thing?
10. Do you admit complaints will enrich business goodwill?
11. Mention four points of sellers argument to refuse complaints.
12. Mention any four view points of buyer as an aggrieved party.
13. Mention four points of hinting on writing adjustment letters?
14. For delay in despatch of goods, mention any two admissible reasons?
15. Sketch out a letter head in complaint letter of your imagination.
16. Give the complimentary close in a complaint letter for supply of inferior quality goods.
17. Do you accept apology and submission in seller's reply ?
18. Do you admit of complaint due to customer's ignorance?

12 Marks Questions

1. Crystal sugar company of Hiriyur has got a complaint from sweet seller at Tiptur that grade of sugar implied in the order is ignored. Draft both the letters of complaint and reply.
2. Chamatkara Cement Works of Durgapur has sent you seventy bags of very poor quality of cement unfit for use in construction of a bridge, as a contractor–buyer lodge a complaint and also a convincing reply on behalf of the supplier.
3. Dignity plastic company in whitefield, Bangalore, receives a complaint from colour plastics dealer of Basavanagudi regarding delay in despatch of the order. Write a suitable reply.
4. LYKA Medicine manufacturer of Bombay is said to have supplied drug of no avail for cough treatment. As a seller you have received abundant local complaints. It is said to be highly allergic. Draft a sensible and seriously worded complaint letter.
5. As a customer of cosmetics when you visited superb cosmetic showroom at Mysore, you were not cared for when you demanded an explanation for abuse of some beautifying element in the manufacture of cosmetics. Address a letter of complaint to sales compaign section of the concerned company.

6. Inspite of clear mention of designs and sizes of shirts for children and adults in your order to dependable stores of Davangere, from the consignment sent to you. You ascertain that only double consignment. Write a letter of complaint for wrongly sent goods and put forth a condition for retention of already consigned goods only if seller agrees to allow you a discount of 7 to 10%.

7. Tension proof Nylon guts manufacturing firm in Bangalore receives a letter of complaint written in a fit of temper and incivility from a buyer in Tumkur. Write a perfect and acceptable reply to rebut his charges in a rational manner.

*****

CHAPTER 5

SALES CORRESPONDENCE

- Definition
- Trade Reference and Status Enquiries

Circular letters are sent to all the customers at the same time. The commonest circular letter is the notice of a meeting sent to members. Circular letter is ideal when the same message is to be conveyed to numerous people. In such cases, the circular letter saves enormous amount of time, money and energy. Mass production therefore characterises a circular letter.

Numerous occasions warrant issue of circular letters. A letter inviting members to a meeting is a circular whether it is in the form of a notice or in the form of a letter. The Sales Manager can periodically write circular letters to his salesmen or agents spread over a wide geographical area. Trade Associations, Chambers of Commerce, etc., keep their members informed of the developments in commerce through circulars. A manufacturer can use the circular letters to introduce a product or in support of a sales campaign. Assumption of a new agency, sale of a business, grant or withdrawal of a certain authority, dissolution of a business, significant changes in the policy of a firm, change in the constitution of an organisation, opening of new branched establishment of a new business, etc., can be conveyed effectively through circular letters.

A circular letter binds the signatory as much as any other letter does. Thus, circular letters cannot be used to make promises one cannot keep. Although they are generated *en masse* they should not look cheap. Although a good-looking circular letter does not in itself guarantee spectacular results, a bad circular letter is sure to attract adverse publicity.

1. Shifting to a new premises

Specimen 1:

Phone : 22347612

RAMADOOT OIL EXPORTERS LTD.,
No. 35, 6th Cross, Malleswaram,
Bangalore - 560 003.

June 7, 2006

Dear Customers,

We are happy to inform you that our business has grown with the best wishes and good feelings of our customers. This has made us to move to a larger premises. The present premises is too small to be able to produce sufficient goods to meet the growing demand. With the object of providing good service to our customers we have taken a new spacious premises at No. 9, Prabath Complex, Kempegowda Road, Bangalore........

The new premises is easily accessible by road. In this premises, better work environment is created to employees. Some works are mechanised. Sophisticated office equipment are provided to have efficiency in business operations. Trained employees are posted to this office with a view to providing good service to customers. Customers service cell is an added attraction in this premises. You are looked after well regarding your business dealings. You can contract this cell for solving your business problems concerning our firm.

As the shifting is in progress, the working schedule is slightly affected. The shifting will be complete within one week and we request you to bear with us for the inconvenience that may be caused to you during this period.

Mr. Raja Ram has been appointed as the Manager of this new office. The office works between 9 a.m. and 5 p.m. with a break of one hour between 1 p.m. and 2 p.m. for lunch.

I take this opportunity to invite you to the opening ceremony on 15-6-2006 and thank you for your good patronage. We hope to render better service in future.

Yours faithfully,
(Sd) General Manager.

2. **Opening of a New Department:** In this circular, information about the functioning of a new department is given. Usually, it contains the date of opening the new department, its location in the business premises, its functions and any other special issue connected with the business. The need for expansion with an explanation is also given in this type of letter.

Specimen 2: Opening a New Department

ROYAL BOOK SELLERS LTD.,
No. 20, M.G. Road, Bangalore - 1.

10-6-2006

Dear Customer,

We bring to your kind notice, that we are opening a separate sales counter to supply B.Com. books to our students and customers. The growing demand for B.Com. books has made us to take this pleasant step. The new counter will have both retail and wholesale sections.

Books are classified according to the subjects. The customers can have an easy access to any book they need. Our sales persons will be happy to guide you to purchase the book you want. All new titles are displayed at the entrance.

The manager of this section is Mr. Raghuram, who holds a Master's Degree in Commerce and a Diploma in Marketing Management. He has 5 years of selling experience. He will be at your service and guide you regarding the books you need. This facilitates you in selecting the right book.

The new counter will open on June 15, 2006 in our business premises at 10 a.m. Your are cordially invited to this function. Please feel free to visit this counter at your convenience to select the best books on commerce and management.

I thank you for your good patronage.

Yours Sincerely,
(Sd) General Manager.

3. **Renovation of the Premises:** When the renovation of the existing building takes place, the customers are put to hardship. The regular business operations are affected. There may be the closure of business for some time. These are to be informed to the customers well in advance and they should be requested to bear with the firm for delays and inconveniences caused to them during this period. The following specimen will help you to draft a circular regarding the renovation of premises.

Specimen 3: Renovation of Premises

SHILPA COMPUTERS LTD.,

No. 10, 1st Gross,
Gandhinagar,
Bangalore - 560 009.
June 15, 2006

Dear Customers,

The growing demand for our business has necessitated to renovate our existing premises. We have to make certain alterations in the work place to have more space and to instal two more computers to meet the existing demand. With this end in view, we are renovating the building. Atleast two months are required to execute the job. We are closing our premises from July 1, 2006 for two months. During this period, the business operations will take place in the adjoining building. Customers are requested to co-operate with us in completing this task.

We regret for the inconvenience caused to you temporarily and request you to overlook the matter.

Yours Sincerely,
For Shilpa Computers.

4. **Opening a New Branch:** In announcing the opening of a new branch, it is necessary to include the opening date, the address (which should be displayed) and the name of the branch manager. In many cases, instructions for future *cor* respondence are also given.

Specimen 4: Opening a new branch

SHESHACHAL TRANSPORT SERVICE
No. 9, Sira Gate, Tumkur

June 20, 2006

CIRCULAR

Dear Customer,

We are glad to announce the opening of a new branch at M.G. Road Tumkur, for the convenience of our customers in the city. Our MG. Road Branch office will be stationed at

No. 15, M.G. Road,
(Next to Mahadev Variety Stores)
Tumkur.

It is spacious and we shall provide safe place for the customer's parcels. Besides providing the facilities in the main office, we have also made special arrangement for safe handling of oil goods and glasswares.

Sri. Nataraj is our manager of that branch and is well know in that area. He will be at your service to solve your transport problems.

You are invited to visit the branch on the opening day, 1st July, 2006 at any time between 8 a.m. and 8 p.m.

I thank you for your patronage and assure you that we shall always make every effort to give continued satisfaction.

Yours Sincerely,
For Sheshachal Transport Service,
(Sd) General Manager.

Group B

Circulars relating to Partnership Firm

There will be constitutional changes in the partnership firms, such as admission of a partner, retirement of a partner, amalgamation of firms, or sale of the firm to a joint stock company. When the customers have reposed confidence in the operations of the firm, these structural changes may develop of a diffidence in the minds of loyal customers. In order to instil confidence in them, information will be sent through circulars. The customers will come to know of the circumstances in which the changes have taken place. They also feel that their interest in the firm will not be affected due to these changes.

If a partner is admitted to the firm, the firm will try to project his image as a partner in the firm. The circular letter drafted in this connection will inform the customers and others interested in the firm, the ability of new partner, his capital contribution, the benefit the firm would derive by his admission, etc., His specimen signature will also be circulated as a piece of information to the customers. The following specimen will help you to understand the implication of this type of circular.

Specimen - 5

Phone : 608478

RAMESH (P) LTD.,

No. 25, 17th Cross Malleswaram, B'lore - 3

June 1, 2006

CIRCULAR REGARDING ADMISSION

Dear Customer,

Your continuous patronage to our firm has encouraged us to expand our activity. As we need additional capital and managerial power we have admitted Mr. Raghuveer as our partner.

Mr. Raghuveer has been associated with the business in various capacities for the past ten years. His knowledge in the business will be better utilised as a partner. He has contributed his share of capital which will suffice the additional capital.

The firm continues the business under the same name and style and there will be change in any policy of the firm.

The specimen signature of Mr. Raghuveer is given below :

Your continued support is solicited.

Specimen Signature

....

(Mr. Raghuveer)

Yours Sincerely,

For Ramesh (P) Ltd.,

(Sd) Ramesh.

Specimen 6: Retirement of a partner

This type of circular starts with an expression of regret and an appreciation of service the retiring partner has rendered to the firm. Customers normally will have confidence in a partner and if that partner retires, the customers are likely to lose confidence. Therefore, the firm should assure the customers that the gap is filled by appointing another manager or admitting another partner of equal competence. The letter should contain the goodwill message and a request for future co-operation.

MADHU MALATHI ENTERPRISES

No. 15, K.R. Extension, Tiptur

July 10, 2006

Dear Customer,

We regret to inform you that our managing partner Mr. Madhu, has retired from business for health reasons from 1st July 2006. We record with a deep sense of gratitude the service he has rendered to our firm. However, he continues to be an adviser of the firm which will help us in running the business on sound lines.

Sri. Gopalan, has been appointed as the General Manager of the firm who has been entrusted with the task of carrying out all the work Mr. Madhu was doing. Mr. Gopalan has worked as a manager in a firm doing identical business for 5 years. His rich knowledge in the field will prove immensely useful to our firm.

We request you to extend your unstained co-operation in the changed circumstances of the firm.

Yours faithfully,
For Madhu Malathi Enterprises,
(sd) Malathi

Similar letters are drafted when there is amalgamation or sale of firm. However, the following points are to be incorporated whenever such circulars are drafted.

(i) Give an announcement of constitutional change in the firm.

(ii) Incorporate the effects of such changes in the firm, and also the change of partner.

(iii) A sentence to infuse confidence amongst the customers and suppliers.

Group C

New Business

Circulars are also issued when a new business is established. New. business may be in the form of (i) Establishing a new business (ii) Purchasing an on going business (iii) Acquiring an agency.

(i) Establishing a new business: When a new business is started, the proprietor of a firm will have to give a wide publicity about its operations. Customers will already have a business preference. In order to attract these customers, certain concessions have to be shown in the initial stages. Incorporating these concessions a circular has to be drafted. The circular should also include the profile of the firm. This means, the knowledge of the trade the firm has, the capital invested, the policies of the firm etc., are to be included. An appeal to the prospective customers should also be made. The following specimen will help the reader to know the type of circular to be drafted.

Specimen 7: Circular regarding establishing a new business

GEETHA VARIETY CENTRE
Bus Stand, Tiptur.

5-9-2006

Dear Customer,

Owing to the growing demand for stationery and fancy articles, ascribable to increase in student population in the town, we are motivated to establish a variety centre under the name and style "GEETHA VARIETY CENTRE" at G.K. Complex, Bus Stand, Tiptur.

Our store deals in all varieties of stationery articles, fancy goods and school books. We have a special sales counter for school children. The salesman is experienced ir dealing with buyers and you will have a happy time when you visit with your children.

Our pleasing sales persons in different counters take care of your needs and you will enjoy your purchases with us.

Keeping in view the customer satisfaction, we have adopted the new price policy slightly competitive in character.

We have introduced credit card system coupled with door delivery. We are pleased to deliver your stationery requirements at your door steps, if you have an arrangement with us.

Our phone Number is 253194. Please visit us to know more of us.

With best wishes.

Yours sincerely,
For Geetha Variety Centre,
Ranjan (Partner).

(ii) Purchasing On-Going Business: The change in ownership of an established firm needs only the introduction of new owner to the customers. When there is a takeover, there may or may not be change in the business policy of the firm. If any change is effected, it should also be brought to the notice of the customer. The ability, strength and business knowledge of the new owner should be highlighted in the circular, which wins the confidence of the customers. If the business is a reputed one, the new owner can continue the business without making much change in the business policy. The circular should also bring to the notice of the customers that new owner has sufficient capital to run the business uninterruptedly. A letter of the seller informing the sale is normally attached to the circular. Specimen signature of the purchaser should also be incorporated in the circular.

Specimen 8:

KIRAN JEWELLERY (P) LTD.,
No. 15, Avenue Road, Bangalore -2

June 15, 2006

Dear Customer,

We are happy to inform you that 'Kiran Jewellery' is taken over by us.

We continue to run the business under the same name. As the policies of the firm are successful, we have no intention to change any policy. We shall put in every effort to maintain the tradition of excellent service that this business stood for.

As the owners of reputed 'Sriram Jewelleries' we are aware of the Jewellery business for a long time. We have also adequate resources at our command to meet any business challenge of the newly acquired business.

We have evolved a new scheme of easy purchase, the details of which can be had from the shop during working hours.

Only your continued business with us will tell you the efficient service that we render you as before. We assure you that you will feel satisfied when you visit us.

With seasons greetings and best wishes.

Yours sincerely,
For Kiran Jewellers,
(sd) Kiran Kumar.

(iii) Acquiring an Agency: A circular relating to the acquisition of an agency should contain information regarding the product, price, sales policy of the firm, the field experience the agent has and the services he is extending to the customers. If the product is a new one, he should give the product profile. If the product has already developed a brand loyalty, the agent should only ensure the uninterrupted supply of the product to the customer. Observe the following specimen:

Specimen 9: Agency Circular

PROMPT AGENCY SERVICES

No. 1658, 1st Cross, Gandhinagar, Bangalore - 560 009.

June 8, 2006

Dear Customer,

We are happy to inform you that we have been appointed as selling agents in your territory for "health care products" manufactured by "Colgate- Palmolive".

Colgate - Palmolive products are highly rated products in the market and we are very pleased to sell them in your area. The company has the standard sales policy which has been accepted by the customers over the years. With a view to ensuring quick delivery of the products to you, the company has thought of opening an agency service in your area.

Prompt Agency Services are known for quick and honest service; and, we are pleased to accept the task of a highly rated company. We assure you the prompt service. The agency house is situated at

No. 10, Gandhi Bazar,
Basavangudi, Bangalore - 560 004.

This agency covers the Basavangudi, Banashankari I, II & III stage, Jayanagar all blocks, Tyagarajanagar residential areas and all the customers in these areas may please contact us for your requirements. Our telephone number is 22603475.

We take this opportunity to thank you for your patronage and request you to continue the same co-operation to M/s Prompt Agency Services.

Yours sincerely,
For Prompt Agency Services,
(sd) Srinivasa.

Thus, regarding new business operations, several types of circulars are issued. However the following essential points are to be borne in mind while drafting such circulars:.

(i) Giving a wide publicity of the estabishment of the new business with details of address, telephone number, types of service rendered, place, etc.

(ii) Complete information about the owner, his ability, experience, capital strength and managerial resources he has, to take-up the task.

(iii) Request for visits. Invitation to the opening ceremony.

(iv) Information regarding the initial incentives given, good will message, assurance to render good service etc.,

Group D

Conversion of a firm into a Company

Some of the firms would like to expand their activities or diversify their business. In such circumstances there will be a greater need for capital and managerial ability. The existing customers may be informed of such conversion through circular letters highlighting the advantages that the customers would get. However, such conversion would affect the customers relationship and hence the circular should be drafted to inform the customers that their relationship with the firm will not affect in any way due to change in the constitution of the firm. The following specimen will help the reader to understand clearly the tone of such letter.

Specimen 10: Circular regarding conversion

RAJAN1 ENTERPRISES

East Park Road, Bangalore - 3

June 15, 2006

Dear Customer,

The partners of the firm, considering the evergrowing demand for the products sold through their firm, would now like to expand the activities of the firm.One of the major activities of such expansion is to manufacture the product. The marketing of that product is not a difficult task as they have good network of branches throughout the country.

Adequate capital is required to expand this activity. Therefore, the management has decided to convert the firm into a public limited company. As soon as the conversion process is over, the company would enter the capital market to mobilise the required finance.

Keeping in view the patronage extended by you, the newly formed company would reserve some shares to be allotted to you on priority basis. The firm also assures that there will not be any changes in traditions of the firm.

The firm earnestly hopes that you will continue to extend your partronage to the newly formed company.

With best wishes,

Yours sincerely,
For Rajani Enterprises
(sd) Managing Partner.

Group E

Other Circulars

There are several other types of circulars issued by the business firms.

They are related to :

(i) Introducing a new product.

(ii) Changes in the policy of the firm.

(iii) Granting or withdrawal of 'per pro' authority.

(iv) Removal of an employee or appointing a person to a key post in the firm.

(v) Company circulars : (a) Meeting Notice (b) Declaration of bonus shares (c) Announcement of Rights issue to the existing share holds (d) circulation of motions or resolutions to be moved in Annual General Meetings.

(vi) Sales letter.

(vii) Follow-up letters.

Specimen circulars are given below relating to some of the above stated matters.

Introducing A New Product :

Circular letter gives identical information to all those concerned–Drafting a circular to convey the message relating to the introduction of a new product by a firm needs extra care. The product should be properly projected in the letter. Its physical features and utility are to be highlighted. The projection should be such that it should create an impelling force in the minds of the readers and they should be prompted to go in for that product. This is more a sales letter than a circular.

We have discussed about the sales letter in the beginning. However, it contains certain message to the target customer which arouses interest in him regarding the product. In order to arouse interest, normally, there will be striking opening statements or proverbs e.g.," Protection of your family is your prime consideration". Or "Every problem has a solution" or the proverbs like" "Every cloud has a silver lining". These sayings create interest in the minds of the prospect. The text of the letter should be such that it will maintain the interest created in the mind of the prospect. A goods sales letter gives facts and figures to maintain the interest in the minds of customers. It should gently lead the prospect from point to point. He should not be pressurised. Lest he should resent. When his interest in the message is retained throughout the letter he will swing into action. Sales letters of quality products should appeal to the two inner forces of the prospect viz., pride and snobbery. This quality appeal may prove very successful as it gratifies the pride of the purchaser who pays a higher price for them.

It is a fact that a product cannot be given free of cost. But still the human weakness is to get some thing free of cost. Hence, a sales letter should contain certain attractive terms. For example, "One tooth brush free along with the purchase of one company size tooth paste tube". Tooth brush as we know, costs Rs.5 to Rs. 8 today, It cannot be given free of cost. But, when an announcement is made, the customer feels that he is getting it free of cost and forgets that the cost of brush is added on in the price of the paste.

Thus, a circular letter drafted to introduce a new product should be creative and contain striking statements, proverbs, anecdotes, eye-catching words, appealing themes and forceful suggestions to swing into action. Some specimen circulars are given below for your understanding.

Specimen 11: Introducing a New Toilet Soap For Women

In this circular the target customer is a lady. Hence, care should be taken to draft a letter in such a manner that it touches the inner feeling of a lady.

Phone : 232869

SOUMYA HEALTH CARE PRODUCTS LTD.

No. 5, Industrial Estate, Rajajinagar, Bangalore - 10

10th June, 2006

Madam,

"DO NOT IGNORE BEAUTY TREATMENT EVEN
IF YOU ARE BORN BEAUTIFUL"

We have a product for you which takes care of your beauty. Skin needs nourishment. "Soumya Sandal" is a toilet soap, specially produced to take care of your beauty.

Soumya Sandal is rich in sandal oil and other ingredients which provide complete and balanced skin food. It repairs the damaged skin tissues, prevents dry, parched and peeling skin. Soumya

Sandal acts quickly and efficiently to revitalise your skin and renew its added texture and lustre.

Soumya Sandal is tested in our well equipped scientific laboratory. All the ingredients are properly blended to enliven the skin wherever applied. Soumya Sandal flushes the skin pores thoroughly, ejects all impurities, cleans your skin to luminous softness, creams it to silky texture. Soumya Sandal creates for you enchanted aroma and sense of perfect case.

Continuous use of Soumya Sandal keeps you fresh and flower soft all day long; all around the year.

Soumya Sandal is a complete beauty treatment.

Our dealers, M/s. Vilasini Enterprises No. 15, Sampige Road, Bangalore will have pleasure of welcoming you to test Soumya Sandal. Please visit them to get your free sample of Soumya Sandal. All we ask is to spare one hour of your precious time to get your sample and a gift too.

Wish you a happy time with us.

Yours sincerely,
For Soumya Enterprises,
(sd) Sanatham

Specimen 12: Introducing Vaccum Cleaner

This product is a domestic appliance and needs attractive circular to catch the minds of the customers. The circular should contain a good product profile and should woo the customers to purchase this product. Phone : 585699

CLEAN ELECTRONICS
No. 25, Mahadevapura Industrial Estate, Bangalore.

July 5, 2006

Dear Customer,

"YOUR HOME IS NOT REALLY CLEAN
UNLESS IT'S A CLEAN "VACCUM CLEANER"

We are happy to announce the launching of our product "Cleanse Vaccum Cleaner". This is a domestic cleaner and is quite useful in picking up dust.

Sweeping and dusting only displace dirt and dust. But do not remove them. So what you really need is a "CLEANSE VACCUM CLEANER". This sucks up all dust and dirt from every nook and corner of your home cleaning it the way no amount of sweeping or mopping can. This machine can remove such material from difficult corners where human access is not easy. And everything else too looks spic and span- from your carpets, upholstry and curtains to even your music system, TV and VCR.

The Cleanse Electronics Vaccum Cleaner is the only vaccum cleaner in India with the following features:

1. No disposable bags are required. This saves the botheration of changing bags frequently and thus, saves cost.
2. Automatic cord retractor. No cumbersome winding of cord is required.
3. A light and portable machine. This can be moved from room to room comfortably. This makes you use it every day.
4. It is sleek and looks elegant. It will go with your decor.
5. The motor has high suction power and also has a dust level indicator which indicates you the time of cleaning the bag.

This is a complete compact unit and has a three year warranty. For demonstration and inspection please visit.

Swarna Electronics
No. 15, Kempe Gowda Road, Bangalore-560 009.

Assuring you the best of our service.

Yours sincerely,
For Clean Electronics,
(sd) Managing Director

Specimen 13:

Launching a Slimmer

As discussed earlier when a new product is to be launched, two important points to be incorporated in the circular are (i) Product profile, (ii) Facilities and incentives given to the prospect. The said product again is a health care equipment which reduces the fat in the human body and when projection of such equipment is made, the health points are to be highlighted. Go through the following specimen:

DHANWANTR1 HEALTH CARE PRODUCTS LTD
No. 25, Visweshwariah Complex
Mahatma Gandhi Road, Bangalore - 560001.

June 25, 2006

Dear Customer,

"HEALTH IS BETTER THAN WEALTH
IF WEALTH IS LOST, SOMETHING IS LOST,
IF HEALTH IS LOST, EVERYTHING IS LOST"

This is for your information that Dhanwantri Slimmer System has been released to the market. We want you to try this system, if you have a bulky body. This is an efficient system for helping you to attain the slim, trim, youthful waistline you want. According to one's saying "every inch you lose around the middle, takes a year off the way you look". Dhanwantri Slimmer System is tremendous equipment to keep you fit.

Dhanwantri Slimmer System can help you 'melt' excess inches off your waistline easier and faster than you ever thought possible. Just ten minutes of simple, non-tiring exercise, followed by twenty minutes of relaxation, is all it takes, plus, of course, your determination to follow the programme every day. If you "cheat" in performing the exercises, then no programme can do much for you.

In just five short days, you will have already slimmed the first 2 to 7 cms off your waistline. And that is only a part of the story.

It you tone up your abdominal muscles with Dhanwantri Slimmer System, you will find that you feel and look younger, to have more energy and vitality than before.

DHANWANTRI SLIMMER SYSTEM is unconditionally guaranteed to give you all these results. You are at liberty to return the Dhanwantri Slimmer System, if you are not satisfied after the trial period of fifteen days for a full refund.

Act now, reduce fat in your body, post to-day, the No-risk trial order form in the self-addressed envelope which is enclosed. You will be surprised to feel the difference in your body within 15 days. Otherwise, your trial will be absolutely free.

With best wishes,

Yours sincerely,
For Dhanwantri Slimmer System,
(Sd) Managing Director.

Thus, circulars issued in connection with the introduction of a new product should catch the mind of the prospect and create a preservation effect' in him. A loose, shabby, lengthy, non-impressive circular cannot catch the minds of prospective customer. All care should be taken to project the product in proper perspective. Lest, the product should become a slow moving one. The circulars will have a sales value as they indicate success and development. Therefore, it should contain the following points:

(i) Highlight the problem the prospect has.

(ii) Give the product profile.

(iii) Tell, how the product solves the problem of the prospect.

(iv) Tell, also the incentives given on purchase.

(v) Inform after-sales service policy.

(vi) Give a touching complimentary close.

Besides, the circular or sales letters so far discussed, other circulars as stated earlier, are also prepared and sent to the concerned. Some miscellaneous circulars are produced below:

Specimen 14: Notice of closure of books of a company

CHITRA ELECTRONICS LTD.,
No.75, 80 Feet Road, Gandhinagar, Bangalore.

June 30, 2006

NOTICE

NOTICE is hereby given under Sec. 154 of the Companies Act 1956, that the Register of Members and Transfer Books of the company will be closed from 4th July, 2006 to 14th July, 2006, (both days inclusive).

By order of the Board,
(Sd) S.R. Raju,
Secretary.

Specimen 15: Removal of Salesman

Phone: 22284968, 22284969

JYOTHI PHARMACEUTICALS
No. 10, Mysore Road, Kengeri Town, Bangalore.
TO WHOM SO EVER IT MAY CONCERN

Please take note that Sri H.V. Rajan, who was working as Sales Representative in our firm upto 30th June, 2006, has been removed from this date. We request our customers not to enter into any sort of dealings with him on behalf of our firm. If they do so, they will be doing at their own risk.

Nagesh Rao,
Managing partner,
Jyothi Pharmaceuticals.

Specimen 16: Circular relating to Agency

(i) From the Company :

Ph : Factory : 22367580
Office : 26248896

RASHMI HEALTH CARE PRODUCTS LTD.,
No. 82, Industrial Estate, Rajajinagar, Bangalore - 10

June 25, 2006

TO WHOM SO EVER IT MAY CONCERN

Dear Customer,

Owing to the growing demand for our product SUHASINI SANDAL SOAP, we have appointed M/s. SRIRAM ENTERPRISES, B.H. ROAD, TUMKUR, as our selling agents for Tumkur, Kolar and

Bangalore Rural Districts. We request our customers and retailers of this territory to contact SUHASINI SANDAL SOAP.

We hope that you will extend the co-operation to our agent as you were extending hither to us.

Yours faithfully,
(Sd) Managing Director

(ii) From the Agents:

SRIRAM ENTERPRISES
B. H. Road , Tumkur

June 30, 2006

Dear customer,

We announce with great happiness that we have been appointed as sole selling distributors for the product SUHASINI SANDAL SOAP manufactured by Rashmi Health Care Products Ltd. Bangalore - 10. You need no introduction of the product as it is a very popular brand and manufactured by the reputed health care comapny.

We wish to state that we keep sufficient quantity of soaps and request our dealers and consumers of Tumkur, Kolar and Bangalore Rural District to purchase Suhasini Sandal.

We assure you the best of our services at all times.

Yours faithfully,
For Sriram Enterprises,
(Sd) Sriram.

Specimen 17: Withdrawal of Power of Attorney

KARNATAKA TEXTILES LTD.
No. 10, Magadi Road, Bangalore - 560040.

15-6-2006

TO ALL IT MAY CONCERN

Please take note that M/s. Aswini Real Estate Agents, No. 10, I Cross, Gandhinagar, who were holding the Power of Attorney to sell, mortgage, have contracts on behalf of us, regarding site and building therein at No. 10, 15th Main 10th Cross, Basaveshwarnagar, Bangalore, has been withdrawn. M/s Aswini Real State Agents cease to be Attorney from 1 June 2006, for purpose referred to above.

Any person, entering into any type of contract or any other dealing relating to the said property of firm, from June 2006, will be doing at their own risk. Our firm Karnataka Textiles Ltd., is not responsible for any such dealings.

(Sd) Shesha Murthy,
Managing Director.

Advantages of Circulars:

Circular letters have several advantages:

(i) Identical information can be communicated to a large number of people who are concerned with such information.

(ii) It is a mass communication letter and reaches all the concerned with less effort.

(iii) There will be a personal touch in the letter. A well drafted circular makes the reader feel satisfied as it plays the role of message giver.

(iv) It is less expensive..

(v) It creates a preservation effect which a representative cannot do.

(vi) The information can be read at the convenience of the customer.

Specimen 18: Swajay India Ltd., notifies its members that some registers/books of the company will remain closed during a certain period.

SWAJAY INDIA LTD

NOTICE

NOTICE is hereby given under Section 154 of the Companies Act, 1956 that the Register of Members and the Transfer Books of the company will be closed from Wednesday, 24th December 2005 to Monday 5th January 2006, both days inclusive.

Dated: 3rd December 1997.

By order of the Board,
S. Bhaskar,
Secretary.

Registered Office:
582, Garden Reach, MUMBAI; 400 001.

Specimen 19: Gowda & Gowda inform their patrons that they are moving to new premises.

GOWDA & GOWDA,

312, Mission Road,

BANGALORE: 560 027.

08/06/2006

Tel: 2228 4532

Dear Patrons,

We are pleased to inform you that we are moving to new premises @ # 261, Green Villa, Mission Road, Bangalore: 560 027 on 15th August 2006. The modern, spacious premises will help us serve our patrons better. Our telephone numbers will remain unchanged.

Yours truly,
(R. Ninge Gowda),
Authorised Signatory

Specimen 20: A company notifies that their Sales Officer has left.

NOTICE

THIS IS TO INFORM ALL CONCERNED THAT MR. H. T. SINGHANIA, OUR SALES OFFICER HAS LEFT OUR SERVICE AND IS NOT AUTHORISED TO REPRESENT US HEREAFTER.

Authorised Signatory

GOWDA & GOWDA,
312, Mission Road,
BANGALORE: 560 027.
JULY 25, 2006

Specimen 21: Circular to customers notifying the opening of new premises and an alteration of the address of the company's Registered Office.

DACOSTA & DACOSTA LIMITED

#524, Madame Cama Road,
Mahim,
Mumbai,
08/06/2006

Dear Sir,

Our Directors have been compelled to seek larger premises for the productive side of our organisation as a result of the great development of our business during the past year. They have been fortunate in securing a factory that will be ideal for our purposes and will enable us to supply the latest equipment promptly.

We shall begin operations at the new premises on the 15th August next and as the Registered Office is being transferred in conjunction with our manufacturing establishment, all communications as and from the 14th August should be addressed to the Company at: #142, Joshiwada, Thane West, District: Raigad, Maharashtra.

Thanking you,

Yours truly,
For Dacosta & Dacosta,
(Sd) (R.N.Narlikar).
Authorised Signatory

Specimen 22: Banerji & Banerji write a letter to an old customer from whom no order has been received for a considerable time.

BANERJI & BANERJI,
#231, Tolly Gunj,
Kolkata: 700 026.

08/06/2006

Mahalingam & Sons,
543, Pycrofts Road,
CHENNAI - 600 067.

Dear Sir,

We have recently been through our records of customers and are sorry to find it is a considerable time since we received an order from you.

As we have had no complaint about goods supplied to you, we assume that they must have given you complete satisfaction. It is possible, however, that you have felt some dissatisfaction of which you have not informed us. If this is so, we should be very glad to have an opportunity of looking into the matter, as our motto is to carry out fully the wishes of our customers.

We have recently extended our business and taken up several new lines. Our new list, which we enclose, will indicate to you that we are supplying the best goods at reasonable prices. Some of the lines offered are real bargains.

We sincerely hope that we shall soon have the pleasure of executing your renewed orders, to which we shall give our utmost care.

Thanking you,

Yours truly,
For Banerji & Banerji,
Authorised Signatory.

Specimen 23: Balu Garments announce the opening of two new branches in Bangalore.

BALU GARMENTS

3765, Richmond Road,
Bangalore - 560 001,
08/06/2006

Dear Sir,

We have great pleasure in informing you that we are opening two new branches on the 15th August, at the following addresses:

26, Mission Road, Bangalore - 27.
24, M.G.Road, Bangalore - 1.

At both of these, all our well known goods will be on sale and in addition, several extremely useful novelties will be displayed at reasonable prices.

Our managers at the new branches will be very pleased to welcome you and to show you round the premises. They will also be glad to let you examine any article in stock.

Yours truly,
For Balu Garments,
(S.S.BALU)
Authorised Signatory.

Specimen 24: Letter from Bread & Butter Ltd., on the eve of introducing a new product.

BREAD & BUTTER LTD.

Plot No: 434,
Industrial Estate, Shimla,
08/06/2006

Dear Sir,

Our new season's pack of strawberry jam has now received its final testing and is ready to appear upon the market. In spite of slightly increased costs, we are making no advance in price at the moment, although our present quotation is subject to alteration after the 30th September 2006.

The strawberry crop in this district fell below the average in quantity but was unusually of high quality. Fully 75% of our berries are now from "Empress" plants that yield fruit giving an excellently flavoured jam of an unusually fine colour.

We hardly need to say that our reputation for purity and cleanliness has been fully maintained and the utmost care has been taken to ensure that only the finest cane sugar and fresh whole fruit are used.

Our prices for this superfine jam are:

500 Gm. Glass jars, per doz. Rs. 512/-
1000 Gm. Glass jars, per doz., 970/-,

subject to our usual terms.

In view of our rapidly increasing business, we strongly recommend our old clients to contract for their estimated requirements in advance. Deliveries can be made at any specified dates, in lots of one case upwards carriage paid, and by ordering early you are assured of delivery at the dates required, of any quantity you may desire. Our last season's pack was completely sold out four months ago, so that only those who contract for their requirements can be certain of ample stocks throughout the year.

We hope to receive your orders at the earliest possible moment, in order that punctual delivery may be ensured. An extensive advertising campaign begins on Monday next and we confidently anticipate a record season.

Yours truly,
For Bread & Butter Ltd.,
Deepak Pershad,
Director.

To conclude the discussion on circular and sales letter, while drafting these letters, the following points have to be borne in mind:

Circular Letters :

(i) It is a mass-based letter and hence, it should have a wide coverage.

(ii) The letter should be brought to perfection after revising several drafts.

(iii) Consult your colleagues in the firm who know the good drafting and bring out a final draft.

(iv) If need be, consult the experts before it is released.

(v) Carelessness on the part of the person who drafts the letter may irritate the reader. Hence, be careful and use good language.

(vi) Any flaw in the letter will be magnified by the number of copies. Therefore, carefully read the draft and avoid mistakes.

(vii) Have a personal touch in the letter, do not be disrespectful.

(viii) Avoid promises which you cannot keep; do not exaggerate; do not trick the customer.

(ix) Let the salutation be pleasing.

(x) The opening paragraph should be attractive. It can also open with striking statements or proverbs.

(xi) The body of the letter should sustain the interest of the reader.

(xii) The closing paragraph should end with a forceful suggestion for immediate action.

Trade Reference and Status Enquiries

'Trade' implies purchase and sale. If cash is paid to buy the goods, the deal will be safe and complete. But in the world of trade, the position is not always as secure and systematic as we often desire. Customers buy goods and pay for it at a subsequent stage. A specified date, end of week/month may be agreed upon. Here also if the amount is settled by paying cash, there is no room for anxiety. But unlike in the past "pay cash and carry" or "cash to-day, credit tommorrow", credit has penetrated and devoured the arena of modern business to a greater extent. If cash deal alone were a pre-condition to the business-transaction, the gamut of modern business would not have reached the global pinnacle. If cash implies periodical payment, reckless credit-granting would harm the financial position of the seller. In the past, credit was a taboo, seldom asked and rarely given. But today traders have to follow a believe policy of granting credit. The structure of business is built upon mutual trust. A substantial part of business is conducted on credit. Credit is the life blood of trade and industry. Credit promotes business. Credit may increase business profits, if properly planned. The great majority of traders meet their obligations honestly but, reasons or mental tension are (a) dishonesty (b) insufficient captial and (c) undue risk. Even then, sale of goods on credit in business is common practice today. Therefore, to minimise the risk which is inherent in supplying goods on credit, the prudent trader will always make inquiries as to the standing and credit of any new customer who wishes to order goods in this way. Bad debts and delayed payments will be the risk factors in case of credit transactions. Just increase in sales does not mean easy realisation. Collection or timely repayment is a matter of difficulty and costly affair too. It is a two way sharp blade. It involves name also. A very efficient policy of sanctioning credit should aim at minimising bad debts, easy repayment by customers and peak sales.

The four C's to be enquired into and confirmed to be are Character, Capacity, Captial and Condition.

Character implies integrity, loyalty, fair deal, bonafide intention, belief, morale, regularity in repayment and worthy habits.

Capacity implies ability, skill, dexterity, experience, know-how, calibre, assessment fund of information and awareness.

Capital implies property, sale price, profit accumulation and proportion between property and obligation to pay.

Condition refers to ease in Trade, macro economic factors in the society which will depend upon business deals routine and specific

Sources of ascertaining customer's financial strength may be enlisted as under:

1. Previous order - Quantity and amount
2. Sales Representative's opinion
3. Personal talk (interview)
4. Profit & Loss A/c and B/S - previous 3 years
5. Names and Addresses of Traders given by customer himself (Referees or Trader References)
6. Names and Address of Bankers- with whom the customer deals (Bank References)
7. Mercantile organisations, chambers of commerce, Inquiry Agencies.

Trade Reference means the names of businessmen mentioned by the credit seeking customer about whom they give some reliable information in a concise and suggestive manner. In their message, they may supplement or supplement the likely pcsitive approach of the seller or any pre-conceived picture about the financial ability and credit worthiness of the customer.

'Bank Reference' means the names of Bankers who guarantee's the customer's potential to the seller to enable the seller to know about his financial position from the bankers.

Both "Trade Reference' and 'Bank References' may not be wholly satisfactory methods of inquiry because of (a) unscrupulous references who might be well known to the customer as friends or relatives and (b) the customer may give only the name of the bank where he has maintained good accounts position so far. Occasions on which customers may give trade reference are (a) Order placement expecting credit-facility and (b) Application for appointment. References may be firms or individual merchants. A prospective customer or an agent will have to give the names of references with their addresses. Any business firm giving credit/ job/agency will expect this from credit buyer/job seeker or applicant/ candidate for agency.

Credit Enquiry Agencies will supply reliable information in respect of business standing, financial capacity, nature of business and the businessman (status and standing) at regular service cells (professional). They charge some amount pre-determined depending upon the nature of service they render.

In case of bank reference, the customer will quote his bank's name and address and the seller in turn, will hand over the details of his customer to seller's bank and finally, the seller's bank will seek the information about the customer from the customer's bank and will pass on the information to its own client, (i.e. seller).

Guidelines for writing letter to customer asking for names and addresses of references or reference:

1. Indicate pleasure for his soliciting credit and say thanks for placing the order.
2. Demand for the credit information in a convincing way.
3. Solicit him to give Trade/Bank Ref/P&L A/c +B/s or attend personal interview.
4. Ensure that information will be kept confidential.
5. Make a mention about good will, prompt furnishing of referee's details in an unambiguous and courteous manner.
6. Don't use harsh, dubious, suspicious and injurious expressions. Don't make him feel that his credit is being questioned. Create an impression in his mind that credit information - provision is a normal matter of Trade.

Specimen 1: Letter asking for references

RUDRA MARTHANDA & CO

62, Parvathi Street,
Veebhuthipura, Tumkur -3
14th January, 2006

MESSRS. PINAKA & CO.,
186, Nrithya Road,
Neelakantapura, TIPTUR - 1.

Dear Sir,

Thank you for your order of 11th January, 2006

Since you are having your every first transaction with us, our trade practice expects you to give us any two worthy references. We follow this trade tradition without fail. Therefore, you please give us the trade-credit information sources without any delay what so ever.

By the time you respond to our trade convention, we will be ready to attend to your order.

We are quite confident that you will encourage us to begin our mutual and new deal with long-standing cordiality between our business.

Yours faithfully,
Rudrass Marthanda & Co.

Specimen 2: Details not given in orders, hence cash payment suggested, reference demanded, if credit wanted:

WARE AND WALK STORES
(Shoes Wholesalers)

18, Chariot Road,
Chamundipua, Bangalore - 16.
16th June, 2006

DIVYA FOOTWEARS,
K.R. Park Road,
(Near Sir, M.V. Statue)
Tumkur - 2

Dear Sir,

We thank you for the order for 250 pairs of 'FN-Slippers-47' in classified measures and patterns. We wish to note that our business with you is quite a new one. In fact, we both have to inaugurate it.

Your letter does not specify the mode of settlement. Bulk purchase trade practice demands 'cash down and carry', when we execute your order for the first time. Probably you would be aware of it. Anyway, you are given liberty to choose either of the following two for mutual interest:

(a) Send a crossed Cheque for the full sum of Rs. 28,825/- (after 1.25% discount).

(b) Draw a cheque in our favour for Rs. 20,000/- and the balance of Rs. 8,825/- C.O.D.

If at all you desire credit and you implied it while placing the orders with us, it is quite to you even now, to furnish us with two mercantile references (usually wholesale firms' names), we will certainly enrol you as our regular credit-purchaser.

Yours faithfully,
For Ware and Walk Stores,
Kshema Shambhu
Manager.

Specimen: 3 Asking for references

MAHA ATA PAATA & SONS
(Dealers in Toys and Games for children)
19, Green Field Road, Madhugiri, Tumkur (Dt.)

Madhugiri
24th Dec, 2006

Ref. No. 142 XM/2-F
Tel No. 01-264890
Gram •. "Playtoys"
MESSRS. DEHAGATHI AND BROTHERS,
143, Sathanthra Road,
N.M.K. Industrial Area, Kolar - 4

Dear Sir,

Thank you for your order for children's toys bearing the date of 20th Dec. 2006. We are prepared to send you the boxes of toys of your choice. But this is your very first order with us. We desire your contract with us very much.

The total transaction amounts to Rs. 25,000/- and you wish to be granted credit for 3 months. Our trade custom is to ask for trade references without any exception. Therefore we hope to get it for our record purpose soon from you. We hope that you will not misunderstand us on this count.

We firmly believe that your customers will very much like our toys specially made for children's attraction and spontaneous gayness.

We are awaiting an early reply,

Yours faithfully,
For Maha Ata Pata & Sons,
(Sd.) Thandeshwar,
Credit Manager.

Specimen 4: Giving references as desired by the seller (Reply to letter No.3)

DEHAGATHI AND BROTHERS
(Toy Traders)

143, Swathantra Road,
N.M.K. Industrial Area,
KOLAR –4
28th Dec. 2006.

Mr. Thandeshwar, Credit Manager,
MAHA ATA PATA AND SONS,
19, Green Field Road,
Madhugiri, Tumkur (Dt.)

Dear Sir,

Thank you for your letter dated 24th Dec. 2006 expressing your readiness to have an open account in your books. As per your trade custom, we are giving below the addresses of three references who are men of mercantile credibility and dignity. In fact, we have our trading with them for over 2½ decades. In fact, we should have furnished it but, some how, it did not strike us. We also have credit dealings with our own buyers. Our references are:

1. Nambike Trading Co.,
   116/A, B.V.K. Iyengar Road, Bangalore - 5.
2. Shamboshankara & Bros. (P) Ltd.,
   426, Uyyele Complex,
   Gandhrvapura, Mysore - 16
3. Kailaspathi Watch Co
   72/3, Harsha Mahal,
   Santhoshapura, TIPTUR - 2

Our Bankers are State Bank of Mysore, Kolar Branch, Kolar -4. In case, you need some more details, please write to us. Since there is heavy demand for Toys and Play Charts, kindly finish your formality as early as possible and grant us credit to expedite the delivery of Toy consignment to us.

Yours faithfully,
For Dehagathi and Bros.,
(Sd) Miss Chathure,
Manager.

Status Enquiry

On the basis of the trade references given by the customer, the seller has to obtain the credit-information regarding the repaying capacity of the customer. The response to such a letter should be kept highly confidential. In fact, it is a matter of mercantile favour done to us. The status enquiry should seek information regarding (1) general credit worthiness (2) the amount of credit sought for and for the specified A ration, does he deserve ? Vagueness has no place here. Writing should never be dubious and circumlocutory, it should be rather direct and pin-pointed communication.

Style for Writing Status Enquiry Letters

In case of trade reference, the seller writes to the customer or his banker to send reference directly about his credit standing. In case of the Banker who is quoted as referee or reference by the customer, the seller has to approach his own banker to get the credit information about the customer from the customer's banker. Because the bankers do not reveal anything concerning the financial dealings as depicted by the account operated by the customer in question. Therefore, in all the letters addressed to the bankers by the sellers and in turn from the banker to banker and banker to seller, the clear details will avoid vague and imperfect response. Too much of clarity and passing judgements should not be expected here.

Specimen 5: Status enquiry letters are to be written as desired in the letters of example no. 4 above. From Address in Maha Ata Pata and Sons, Madhugiri to all the 3 references noted in the letter.

MAHA ATA PATA AND SONS

19, Green Field Road,
Madhugiri (Tumkur-Dt.)
29th Dec, 2006.

Messrs. Nambike Trading Co.,
116/A, B.V.K. Iyengar Road,
Bangalore - 5.

Dear Sir,

CONFIDENTIAL

The firm noted below has desired to open an account with us for Rs. 25,0000, 3 months and has quoted you for reference.

DEHAGATHI AND BROS.
143, Swathanthra Road.
N.M.K. Industrial Area,
KOLAR - 4

Please furnish us the financial position and their repaying capacity.

The information that you may give us will be kept quite confidential.

We always reciprocate your response with a sense of appreciation and willing co-operation. An envelope duly stamped and self-addressed is pinned to this for your reply without undue delay.

Yours faithfully,
For Maha Ata Pata and Sons,
(Sd.) Thandeshwar,
Credit Manager.

Specimen 6: Favourable Reply to Specimen No. 5 in example:

NAMBIKE TRADING COMPANY

116/A, B.V.K. Iyengar Road,
Bangalore – 5
2nd January, 2006

Messrs. Maha Ata Pata and Sons,
19, Green Field Road, Madhugiri.
(Tumkur-DT)

CONFIDENTIAL

Dear Sir,

We have your enquiry dated 20th Dec, 2005. We are happy to state that Messrs. Dehagathi and Bros. are our decade old customers.

To the extent we know, their financial position is sound. They have been punctual in payment. Their dealings indicate their honesty and trust. Their payments to us have sometimes crossed lakhs of rupees. We would have granted them credit in excess of what you have mentioned. They always avail cash discount facility.

Please keep the information secret and we owe nothing to you on this count.

Yours faithfully,
For Nambike Trading Co.,
(Sd.) P. Neelakanteswar,
Credit Manager.

Specimen 7: Unfavourable Reply to letter No.5 (with a change in "From Address" as per previous example No. 4- Read letter Nos. 4 & 5 to know the context of this letter of example No.7)

SHAMBHO SHANKARA AND BROTHERS P√T. LTD

426, Uyyale Complex, Gandharvapura

MYSORE - 16

STRICTLY PRIVATE AND CONFIDENTIAL

Mysore –165

4th Jan. 2006.

Mr. Thandaeshwar,

Credit Manager,

Maha Ata Pata and Sons,

19, Green Field Road,

Madhugiri, (Tumkur-DT)

Dear Sir,

With reference to your letter dated 29th Dec. 2005 we regret to inform you that the firm about which you seek financial information is facing a crisis. Our bills were not cleared by them in time especially last year. We have a hesitation regarding credit- extension. Till the demise of a senior partner, they had straight dealings and honest clearance of dues if any. Owing to the late payment of Bills, we were forced to discontinue their business with us.

Better you prefer 'cash' to 'on account' deals.

Please treat this fully confidential. We have written this as a (course of business) customary provision of 'What we can say'. This information is quite un-baised and without prejudice.

Yours faithfully,

For Shainbho Shankara and Brothers (P) Ltd.,

(Sd.)

C. Gajacharmamber,

Credit Manager.

Specimen 8: Non-committal Reply to letter No. 5 (with a change in 'From Address' as per previous example No. 4-Read letter nos. 4 and 5 to know the context of Specimen No. 8)

KAILASPATHI WATCH COMPANY

72/3, Harsha Mahal,
Santhoshapura, Tiptur-2
2nd Jan. 2006

CONFIDENTIAL

Mr. Thandeshwar,
Credit Manager,
Maha Ata Pata and Sons.
19, Green Field Road,
Madhugiri (Tumkur-DT)

Dear Sir,

In reply to your letter of 29th Dec, 2005 we regret to inform you that we are not in a position to express an opinion concerning the financial standing and business repute of the firm in question.

Yours faithfully,
For Kailaspathi Watch Co,
(Sd.) A.B. Nagahgeke,
Credit Manager.

Specimen 9: Inquiry through a Banker

BAAHUBALI & CO

16, D.N. Road,
Tumkur –2
23rd March 2006

CONFIDENTIAL

The Manager,
United Commerical Bank of India,
Cottonpet, TUMKUR -2.

Dear Sir,

Messrs. M. Patel and Co., of 16, Chamundi Road, Tumkur-2 propose to avail of credit from us and have given Reference of their bank, Canara Bank, 27, 2nd Cross, III Main, Someswara Extension, TUMKUR-4.

We will be thankful to you if you can inquire into the financial standing and fame of the firm in business and also kindly suggest if it would be alright to sanction them credit to the extent of Rs. 25,000/- 3 months.

Yours faithfully,
Baahubali & Co.

Specimen 10: Reply from the bank

UNITED COMMERCIAL BANK OF INDIA

Cottonpet,
Tumkur -2.
29th March, 2006.

CONFIDENTIAL

Messrs. Baahubali & Co.
16, D.N. Road, Tumkur -2

Dear Sir,

In reply to your letter of 23rd March, 2006 please note that it is contrary to the Bank's custom to inform any body about our customer's financial picture. Hence, route your request through your banker to expect any reply from us.

Yours faithfully,
for UCO Bank,
XYZ
Manager.

Specimen 11: Seller as a customer of XYZ Bank will write a request letter for credit information about Mr. B whose Banker is MNO. Hence, from a seller to XYZ - a request to fetch him credit information about Mr. B from 'MNO' Banker.

SUSHRAVYA RADIO MANUFACTURING CO.,

172, Akasha Extension,
Agrahar, Bangalore –28
18th Sept, 2006.

The Manager
XYZ Bank,
Agrahar Branch,6 Bangalore -28.

Dear Sir,

Messrs Alankara and Co., Radio Sellers, K.G. Street, Koratagere has sent us their order for the supply of My-Transistors No. 24" amounting to Rs.60,000 for 3 months credit.

They have given reference of their Bankers "MNO" Reverse Road Koratagere to obtain information concerning their credit-standing.

If you are able to provide us with any relevant data on their financial soundness and marketing repute, we will be grateful to you. Their estimated orders are stated to be around Rs. 75,000 per quarter of the year.

We solicit your timely information. You are free to advise us.

Yours faithfully,
For Sushravya Radio Mfg. Co.,
Miss. A. Sundari,
Credit Manager.

Specimen 12: A favourable reply to letter No. 11 given above.

XYZ BANK

Head Office : Samudra Theera

Agrahar -Branch, BANGALORE -28

Bangalore –28
27th Sept, 2006.

The Credit Manager,
Sushravya Radio Mfg Co.,
172, Akasha Extension,
Agrahar.
Bangalore - 28.

CONFIDENTIAL

Madam,

Just now, we have got the credit information about the firm you have named in your enquiry letter dated 18th Sept, 2006. Our advise is that the firm has a good name, sound capital structure and plentiful customers. Recently, the firm ventured upon expansion which is a success. They are wholesale dealers also. They have good standing of credit.

This information is for you to use. Please keep this confidential.

The Bank takes no risk or owns any responsibility for information supplied to you or any consequence thereof.

Yours faithfully,
For XYZ Bank,
O.K. Sadachatura,
Manager.

Specimen 13: Unfavourable reply from the bank – (From and To addresses are same us in Specimen - letter No. 12)

Madam,

We had a reasonably good enquiry regarding the firm you named in your letter of 18th Sept, 2006. The enquiry clearly indicates that the firm is stated to have lost its discharging capacity. Liabilities have increased. It is said to be suffering from working capital management problems.

We advise you to be on alert before you part with your stock of goods.

Bank expects you to keep the information highly confidential and the bank renounces itself the possibility of being held subsequently answerable for reliance on the data and potential risk, it any thereof.

Yours faithfully,
For XYZ Bank,
O.K. Sadachandra,
Manager.

Refusal of 'credit' facility to a customer may be sometimes inevitable. Response from the referees may not be favourable. Discourteous message will hurt the customer. Very free and frank refusal of credit is good to say but bad to stay in business. High tone, slang, anger, curt, abrupt rejection, unthoughtful words, utterance etc., will mean a bypath to graveyard of business. Alternative courses of action open to customer should be brought to his notice i.e. (a) Refusal is in his own interest (b) Quantity reduction to and difficulty in payment (c) Offering other services and (d) A word of courtesy to ensure credit, once his financial condition improves.

Specimen 14: Credit Refusal

SUGANDHA SOAP WORKS

Hill Bottoms
J.V. Pura, Bangalore – 52
18th June, 2006.

The Sowgandika Stores,
34, Niraakaara Mandir Road,
Bhootaadhipa Extension,
Tumkur - 4.

Dear Sir,

We are equally hurt to state that the response of referees has been adverse and it does prevent us from giving credit facility to you now.

We firmly believe in your overcoming this tidal depression common to all at one time or the other.

No doubt, even now, if you permit us we will despatch the goods to you C.O.D. We hope our quality goods, reasonably low price and cash discount of 2 1/4% will attract you.

Further clarification except your cash order will not receive our attention.

Yours faithfully,
For Sughanda Soap Words,
V. Hushar,
Credit-head.

STUDY QUESTIONS

Section A

(2 Marks Questions - Answer in 4 lines each)

1. What do you mean by circular letter?
2. Give the meaning of sales letter.
3. State the implications of salutation of a sales letter or circular.
4. What should be the content of opening paragraph of a sales letter?
5. What is a follow-up letter?
6. Mention any two occasions for drafting a circular?
7. What is status enquiry letter?

Section - B

(8 Marks - Answer in 30 lines each)

1. Distinguish between sales letter and a circular.
2. State the contents of a follow-up letter.
3. State the format and contents of a circular letter.
4. Illustrate how a sales letter attracts the reader's attention, arouses his desire, implants conviction and stimulates him into action.
5. "Mass production is the merit as well as the defect of circular letters".
6. Is personal effects seen in circulars? When do you draft such circulars.

Section - C

(15 marks - Answer in 3 pages each)

1. Write a circular letter (sales letter) to introduce any one of the following:

(i) An insecticide	(ii) A refrigerator	(iii) A washing machine
(iv) An Electronic typewriter	(v) A Television	(vi) A Radio
(vii) A Computer	(vii) Industrial goods	(ix) Air Conditioners
(x) Baby Foods	(xi) Talcum Powder, Nail Polish, etc.,	

2. The famous Footwear Centre, who have their main Sales depot at their factory in Tumkur Road, Bangalore, decided to shift their office to Kempegowda Road, Bangalore. Draft a circular announcing the change.

*****

CHAPTER 6

COMMUNICATION & DEVELOPMENT OF THE SKILLS

REPORTS

What is a Report?

C.A. Brown defines report as 'a communication from someone who has some information to someone who wants to use that information.'

Keeping in view the salient aspects we can define a report like this.

'A report is a formal communication written for a specific purpose which includes terms of reference, data collected, analysis of the data, the conclusions, and the recommendations (if necessary).'

Why a Report?

A report serves two purposes. It provides comprehensive, permanent, systematic, clear, and consistent account of a study, an investigation or research. It serves as a tool used for decision-making.

Types of Report

This diagram represents the various types of report.

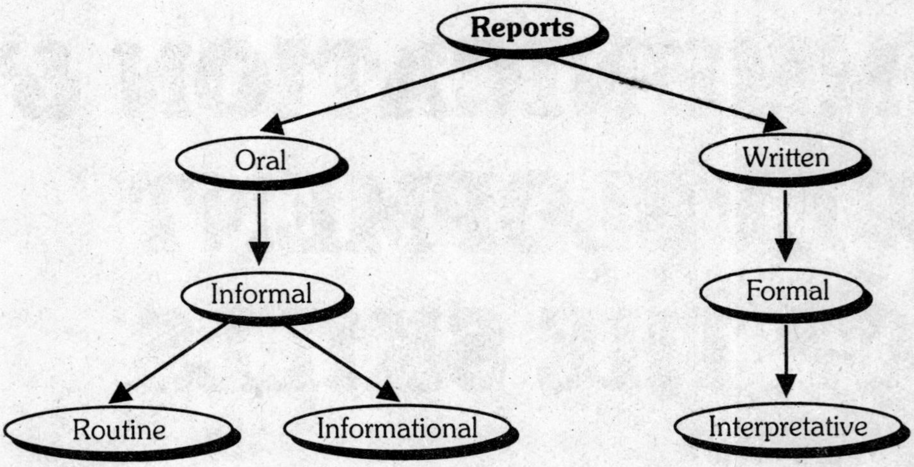

ESSENTIALS FOR EFFECTIVE WRITTEN COMMUNICATION

Knowledge of the essentials helps the writer to make his/her written communication like business of official letters, reports effective and purposeful. Some of them are given here.

1. Clarity

(a) Clarity of thought

(b) Clarity of expression.

2. Conciseness or Brevity

The writer must be economical in words. Written communication may be used as permanent record and, sometimes, often referred to. It is better to be concise keeping in view the reader's valuable time.

To achieve conciseness you can follow these simple rules:

(a) Avoid unnecessary and irrelevant facts

(b) Avoid repetition

(c) Avoid verbosity

(d) Organise the information in logical and coherent manner.

3. Accuracy

Many a time, written communication serves as tool for decision-making and as a legal document and therefore it demands accuracy.

4. Discretion

The written report, sometimes, goes anywhere and is read by anybody and therefore it is necessary for the writer to be cautious. It is better to avoid flippant comments and jokes and take care of the effect on readers.

5. Freedom from Ambiguity

The writer should take care to use right words in right forms at right places.

Syntax, semantics and pronunciation may cause misunderstanding and misinterpretation.

Note: The essentials of effective communication can easily be registered as Six 'C's, viz., clarity, completeness, conciseness, correctness, courtesy, and candidness.

STRUCTURE OF REPORTS

Structure of reports may vary depending upon the kind or type of report. But the outline structure or general framework is maintained while writing reports. Here is diagrammatic representation of the basic structure of a report.

INTRODUCTION

MAIN BODY

CONCLUSIONS

RECOMMENDATIONS [IF NECESSARY]

Organisation of Reports

There are various elements or components or ingredients in a report. It is not necessary that any kind of report should have all these elements. The elements that are necessary for a particular report can be chosen and organised. Mainly, there are three parts, viz., Front Matter, Main Body and Back Matter.

Front Matter

The following elements may be included under this:

1. Cover
2. Frontispiece [illustration facing title-page of book or booklet]
3. Title page
4. Preface
5. Acknowledgments

Mention of thanks to the persons or organisations for the help, co-operation or permissions to use copyright material.

6. Table of contents

Index giving chapter wise or heading wise contents and illustrations.

7. Abstracts and summary (if necessary).

Main Body

This part covers the following elements:

8. Introduction
9. Procedure
10. Findings and Analysis
11. Conclusions
12. Recommendations (if necessary).

Back Matter

This follows the main body and it includes these elements:

13. Appendices
14. List of References
15. Bibliography

This means the titles of earlier reports, or books referred to by the writer(s) to prepare the report.

STAGES IN PREPARATION OF A REPORT

1. Terms of Reference

The work of preparing report starts with the direction or request from the appropriate authority. The report writer mentions this at the beginning as the terms of reference.

A specimen may help you to understand this clearly:

(i) In accordance with your letter No.... dated ... assigning me the work of finding the feasibility of starting a branch of 'National Computer Education Centre' at L.B. Nagar, I am submitting the report that follows.

(ii) In accordance with the resolution at the meeting of the Board of Directors held on .... and the direction from the General Manager in his letter No... dated..., we the following members of the subcommittee are submitting the report on the above-mentioned subject.

2. Assembling the Information or Collecting Data

Information and opinion of both the writer and other concerned or related persons will have to be obtained from various sources. Enough relevant data will have to be collected or gathered from different sources. The report writer should go on collecting and noting down the information, data etc. in his notebook. He has to keep a notebook or diary ready with him during the preparation of a complex report. The writer, later, will have to identify the relevant items which are to be used in his report.

There are various innumerable number of purposes for which the reports are written and obviously there are a number of sources to get the relevant information. Some of the very familiar sources are given below:

(i) Earlier reports

(ii) Personal observation

(iii) Informal discussions

(iv) Proceedings or minutes of meetings

(v) Field work

(vi) Interviews

  (a) Personal interviews

  (b) Telephonic interviews

(vii) Questionnaires

(viii) Visit reports

(ix) Newspaper reports

(x) Reference books.

3. Findings and Analysis

Statistics in suitable tabular form, diagrams, graphs, pictures etc. are to be given at this stage. The writers interpretation or analysis should be given.

4. Conclusion

The conclusions or inferences of the writer should be formed at this stage. This should be examined and re-examined before writing it in the final copy of the report.

5. Recommendations

All reports may not need recommendations. Wherever recommendations are necessary, they should be mentioned clearly point-by-point.

The stages for preparing a report can be diagrammatically represented as follows. This helps for easy grasp and retention in your memory for longer time.

IDENTIFICATION OF PURPOSE

DATA COLLECTION

SORTING OUT RELEVANT DATA

EVALUATION, INTERPRETATION AND ANALYSIS

CHOOSING SUITABLE HEADING AND SUB-HEADINGS

WRITING ROUGH DRAFT

REVISION OR RE-EXAMINATION OF LAY-OUT AND LANGUAGE

FINAL DRAFT AFTER FINE TUNING

Order of Contents

There are normally accepted steps (Headings) to be followed in writing a report. Typical formal report will have the contents in the order given below:

1. Terms of reference
2. Summary
3. Introduction
4. Findings
5. Conclusions

6. Recommendations
7. Appendix

SPECIMEN REPORT

Here is a simple specimen report. This is intended to show the format of a formal report. This serves as broad framework.

(i)

The National Computer Education Centre
38, Temple street, Vikrampur

Sept. 24, 2000

The Managing Director
The National Computer Education Center
Bangalore.

Sir,

Sub: Report on Shifting the Vikrampur Center of NCEC to a New Premises

In accordance with your direction in your letter No.... dated..........., I visited the Vikrampur Center to assess the situation and the progress of the Center. I find that the Center Manager is right in proposing to shift the Center to a better premises.

Present Situation

This center has been functioning at this premises since 1992. Computer Education was not so much popular and the number of students was less. Two new colleges are established, one college of Arts, Science and Commerce and another Polytechnic. The strength of students in these institutions together is around 800. More and more students are showing interest in having computer education. The demand for the various courses in our center here has increased almost threefold. Nowadays, as we know, the infrastructure and show have a major role. The present premises does not give scope either to take more batches or to improve the interior decoration. I agree with the Center Manager in his opinion that the progress of the center will be affected if we continue to function in the same premises.

Merits of the Identified New Building

The new building, viz., 218, Main Road, Vikrampur is situated in the main road. It is very near to the educational institutions, offices and the Bus station. It is a two-storey building with a large hall measuring 20 m x 10m and two rooms 5m x 4m each on the ground floor and the similar accommodation on the first floor. This gives enough scope to arrange for office, counselling cabins, classrooms, practical halls with attractive and congenial interior decoration.

Regarding Negotiations to Secure the New Premises

The owner of the building is Mr. Sharma, a fine man and is well regarded in the town. He has all appreciation for the need and the functioning of our Center. In my discussions with him, I found he is willing to rent out the building to us for running our Center. He is agreeable for the terms — Advance of Rs, 1 lakh and monthly rent of Rs. 6000. Initially it will be leased out for a period of five years and likely to be renewed. I have verified all the records related to the ownership and other encumbrances and found the records all right and the building is free from all encumbrances.

Recommendations

Though the investment in the form of rent and advance seems to be high, I would like to say that our Center Manager has done a good job in identifying this new building and I would like to recommend that the new building should immediately be secured and the Center should be shifted to the new premises. I hope the Center could prosper well and serve better in the new premises.

The detailed estimates for the proposed alterations, interior decoration etc. are enclosed for your perusal.

Yours faithfully,

xyz

(ii) Here is a small report published in a newspaper. The report is on an ordinary and common feature in day-to-day life.

But the reporting is well done. You can see the salient features of a formal report in this small article. Try to read attentively. This serves as an example for how a subject matter can be studied and presented scientifically.

GRATUITOUS GRATUITIES

Everybody loathes it, but everybody does it. A recent poll showed that 40% of Americans, the world's most lavish tippers, hate the practice. It seems so arbitrary, after all. Why does a barman get a tip, but not a fast food worker or a doctor who saves lives? In America alone, tipping is now a $ 16 billion-a-year industry — all the more surprising since it is a behavioural oddity. Consumer acting rationally ought not to pay more than they have to for a given service. Tips, which are voluntary, above and beyond a service's contracted cost, and delivered afterwards, should not exist. So why do they?

The conventional wisdom is that tips both reward the efforts of good service and reduce uncomfortable feelings of inequality. The better the service, the bigger the tip. But according to new research from Cornell University, tipping no longer serves any useful function. The paper analyses data from 2,547 groups dining at 20 different restaurants. The correlation between larger tips and better service was very weak: only a tiny part of the variability in the size of the tip had anything to do with the quality of service. Customers who rated a meal as "excellent" still tipped anywhere between 8% and 37% of the meal price.

Tipping is better explained by culture than by economics. In America, the custom has become institutionalised: it is regarded as part of the accepted cost of a service. In a New York restaurant, failing to tip at least 15% could well mean abuse from the waiter. Hairdressers can expect to get 15-20%, the man who delivers your groceries $2. In Europe, tipping is less common; in many restaurants, discretionary tipping is being replaced by a standard service charge. In many Asian countries, tipping has never really caught on at all. How to account for these national differences? According to Michael Lynn, the Cornell paper's co-author, countries in which people are more extrovert, sociable or neurotic tend to tip more. Tipping relieves anxiety about being served by strangers. And, says Mr. Lynn, "in America, where people are outgoing and expressive, tipping is about social approval. If you tip badly, people think less of you. Tipping well is a chance to show off." Icelanders, by contrast, do not usually tip — a measure of their introversion and lack of neuroses, no doubt.

The hard truth seems to be that tipping does not work. It does not benefit the customer. Nor, in the case of restaurants, does it actually incentivise the waiter, or help the restaurant manager to monitor and assess his staff. The cry of stingy tippers that service people should "just be paid a decent wage" may actually make economic sense.

The Economist
The Times of India, Sept. 8, 2000

Try this Practice Exercise

1. Draft a report as Center Manager of a Computer Education Center on the urgent need and proposal for advertisement campaign.
2. Draft a report as an Academic Director of a reputed Computer Education and Training Center on the need for starting new courses and a software Development Center attached to it.
3. Writer a brief report on 'Noise Pollution, how to Check it?'
4. Write a brief report on 'Keeping the Roads Clean.'

TECHNICAL WRITING AND RESEARCH

Even for technical writing or presentation of research, the framework for report writing given earlier holds good, may be, with a little bit of modifications. The strategies, the stages and the arrangement of contents etc. are almost the same. The steps may be as given under:

(i) Planning your research.

Identifying the main and subsidiary topics or items to be covered, the work schedule like library work, experiments, observation, etc. are to be planned.

(ii) Collection of data or making and storing notes.

(iii) Drafting taking care of the structure of a report.

(iv) Fine tuning and preparing the final report with the necessary contents in suitable order.

Scientific and technical reports, generally, follow the broad framework for preparing reports. Technical paper depends on the topic, the writer, the readership etc.

Specimen Technical Paper

Here is a technical paper. It serves as an example for students to understand and to learn how a technical paper can be prepared for presentation. Please read this attentively and then try to prepare two or three such papers.

Apple's 'Macintosh' line of PCs, rleased in the early 1980s, had hardware capabilities and an operating system with a graphical user interface plus many of the features that Windows 95 has today.

The average PC hardware around 1985, despite phenomenal increase in performance, still wasn't adequate for a hardware-resource-hungry Windows 1.0. Windows 1.0 never took off.

One of the keys to the success of Windows 3.1 was that it ran on top of DOS and used DOS for operations like file access, loading files etc.

Users could therefore avail of both the powerful easy-to-use applications on Windows and the trusted DOS-based applications which they used for several years.

Windows 3.1's support for multitasking was cooperative in nature. This meant that once a task Had begun to run it was up to the task to say to the operating system: "for the moment I don't need the CPU and other computer resources."

In Windows 95 the filenames can be up to 256 characters in length. Therefore, it is possible for a file to be named 'my physics lab work on October 25th 1995.' In DOS one would perhaps have named the file something like 'PHLOCT 25. 195.'

There are many who feel that the integration of many of the programs (which were earlier regarded as applications) into Windows 95, will further reduce competition for Microsoft in the applications market and lead to its total dominance of the deskstop market.

By Vijnan Shastri

Published in the Journal Resonance

Courtesy: The Indian Academy of Sciences Bangalore.

SOME GUIDELINES TO PREPARE TECHNICAL PAPER

Preparation:

1. Begin in defining dearly your objective(s) and your readership.
2. Plan your research
   (a) List out the questions you want to ask
   (b) Make a list of the people and places where you can expect to get the information or answers
3. Schedule your research or study making use of the lists.

Writing the Report

The main items of a report are —

4. A table of contents
5. Acknowledgment (i.e., mention of thanks) when necessary
6. A brief summary
7. An introduction
8. The body of the report
9. Conclusions
10. Recommendations (if necessary)
11. Appendices
12. Bibliography

(Mention of published or unpublished texts quoted or referred to)

PROJECT STUDY AND REPORT

General framework of all types of reports given earlier holds good in preparing a project report. Suitable modifications or change in structure can be made depending upon the nature of project and its readership.

A project report, generally, is expected to have in the beginning some formal certificates, viz.:

(i) Permission to do research or project work and the mention of guide

(ii) Certificate stating it is bonafide research or study

(iii) Declaration by the researchers.

The other stages are almost the same for any type of report. It can be mentioned chapter wise as follows:

Chapter 1. Introduction

2. Objective or Purpose
3. Collection of Data
4. Findings, Analysis and Recommendations if any.
5. Annexures like Pictures, Diagrams, Questionnaires,
6. Bibliography.